D0891690

TIME ON ROCK

TIME ON ROCK

A Climber's Route into the Mountains

Anna Fleming

CANONGATE

First published in Great Britain, the USA and Canada in 2022
by Canongate Books Ltd, 14 High Street, Edinburgh EH1 1TE

Distributed in the USA by Publishers Group West
and in Canada by Publishers Group Canada

canongate.co.uk
1

British Library Cataloguing-in-Publication Data
A catalogue record for this book is available on
request from the British Library

ISBN 978 1 83885 176 7

Typeset in Garamond by Palimpsest Book Production Limited,
Falkirk, Stirlingshire

Printed and bound in Great Britain by Clays Ltd, Elcograf S.p.A

CONTENTS

OPENING

The light is leaving the rock. A great shadow has fallen across the cliff as the sun sinks behind the plateau. The darkness is creeping ever higher up the granite, but at this point on this summer evening, the top of the cliff is burning gold.

If we hurry, we can climb into that light.

Like a pair of ptarmigans, we scuttle down from the plateau, picking our way through loose stones, passing tatty old snow-beds, feet scrabbling through the earth, racing to the foot of the cliff where the rope is swiftly flaked. All forty metres of orange nylon pass through my hands, piling up into a heap on the ground, giving us a clear rope length. I tie into the top end, change shoes and start to work the rock.

The slabs are delicate. My arms and eyes sweep and circle, hunting for holds. Fingers clamp tight around small edges and the grainy crystals bite into my skin. Some edges are friable, crumbling at my touch, releasing a rattle of ancient grit down the rock face. Legs span out for balance and power, toes now pushing down as I step up, the granite demanding the intricate play of tension and release, the opening and closing of mind and muscle.

At a stony bay halfway up the cliff edge, I stop, scanning the weathered features, looking for something secure. A rusty iron peg hangs from the wall – hammered in by some long-forgotten climber. I clip in and build a temporary anchor system from metal and rope, then lean back over to shout,

'Safe!'

The word booms out, echoing off the walls, tumbling down through the vertical space to my partner waiting below. They bound up after me, soon joining me on the ledge, taking the equipment for their part of the climb and then setting off again, swinging out of the stone bay to head up, leaving the shade behind to enter the golden tier overhead.

From my perch, I pay the rope out, watching them shrink into the distance, dwarfed by the rock, the sky and the still evening corrie. Turning on my stance, I look out the other way, and feel that rush of air – the opening of immense space all around us.

A bird cuts across the sky – silent, streamlined, sunlit – the peregrine briefly circles our patch of corrie before moving on to other haunts.

A cry breaks the silence. My partner has reached the top. I dismantle the anchors and step out onto the face again, this time adhering to the edge line where distance soars. My focus is fixed on the immediate stony matter but still my eyes slide, from time to time, off the rock, tumbling out over the edge to take in the monumental scale of mountain space. Beyond my fingertips I glimpse a glacial trough, another vast mountain form and beyond that reams of smaller blue hills melding into the paling sky. I climb on the cusp.

And then I cross the line.

Inside the light, the rock is illuminated, the lichens glowing green and white, the granite softening into warm tones of pink, orange and yellow. I press higher up the sweeping, steepening slab, the sunset mountain opening around me as I move with the rock, toes padding, pressing into the crystalline friction.

—

When I set out to learn the craft of traditional climbing, I had not anticipated how the practice could set places alight. The raw, visceral immediacy of climbing – all the fear, joy, thrills and focus – brings the most intense experience of place. On the rock, surprising connections can be forged between mind, body and landscape. Such close physical contact can offer moments of profound intimacy. Sinking into the rock, the self is lost to movement and environment.

Running alongside that intensity of experience, weaving in and out of the sensations and insights, is a seam of rich culture. Stories, names, histories and characters are always part of the climb and so the layers build up, giving those distinctive rocky spots the most mesmerising depth. Climbing can thus provide a direct route into the spellbinding potency of place.

In these pages I offer an insight into my journey onto the rock – a sometimes hesitant and fluctuating route that took me from being a terrified novice to a competent leader. I share this story not because I have achieved anything ground-breaking but because the process of learning to climb in the outdoors can be transformative. And the simplest way for me to show the nature of that transformation is through my own experience.

Climbing has changed my relationship to the natural world. Picking up a rope and rack and trying to make your way safely up rock faces exposes you to many new experiences. In the vertical landscape, complacency is displaced. You must be present and attentive. The physicality of the activity demands that you learn to handle both the rock and yourself in relation to that rock. In the process, the self changes, adapting to fit around the geological formations.

Climbing can be frightening and demanding, but there is also a beauty within the movement. It is a question of timing, precision and agility. A form of dance. And within that absorbing outdoor ballet – when stretching and balancing, reaching and releasing – you come to see things differently. In the climbing moment, the rock demands your absolute attention. You peer in close, hunting out the cues that lie within the stone, searching for the clues that will help you to solve the puzzle. Then the sequence draws to a close, you relax your gaze and look out – wider. You have climbed to a natural vantage point and from here you gain another perspective. Sweeping views open over the surrounding area. You watch birds circle or survey insects humming above a canopy of trees. You gaze across a mountain landscape, listening to its many voices, feeling your place within that larger scheme. Climbing can give you a new lens. It has widened my focus and deepened my engagement with the natural environment.

This book follows two intertwined journeys. One is the story of my growing ability as a climber. I show how I took to the ropes, learning the techniques and gaining the skills to handle the rock, while also becoming more absorbed in the history and culture of the pursuit. The other is a journey into the rock. As my craft developed, I found that climbing brought an altered perspective, changing my relationship with the natural world. Climbing opened up something – offering a unique way into the landscape – and once I happened upon this opening, I sought to explore it further, by moving out into new environments, different rock types and bigger landscapes.

The chapters follow my route around the UK through my twenties. In this period, my life took a northerly trend, leading from Wales to Liverpool, Yorkshire and Cumbria and then over the border into Scotland. On the way, I grew familiar with many distinctive regions and formed bonds with a variety of people, rocks and landscapes – many of whom have found their way into these pages.

Through intensive physical, emotional and creative work on the rock face, a climber can begin to sense the choreography and movements of land. We see in shapes, patterns and sequences; we place ourselves within rhythms of time, weather and geology. To spend time on rock is to be immersed, orientated and transported.

I

PEAK DISTRICT

GRITSTONE

Adam and I walk up a steep sunken lane where sycamore leaves meet overhead. The sun is shining and the sky is blue but a slight chill hangs in the air. Autumn draws near. My bag is heavy, pressing into my shoulders and lower back, weighing on my calves. I warm up and strip down to a T-shirt. We pass farms and stone cottages. A BMW brakes: we clamber onto the verge to let it pass. The nettles are dusty and tired.

Higher up, the hedge banks lower and I get my first glimpse of the rock. Hen Cloud holds the skyline.

Like an ancient fortress, the outcrop perches atop the hill. Bracken smothers the slopes leading up to the black and red walls. The rock looks proud, distant and formidable. But appearances can be deceptive. Beneath the hard exterior, there may be a way in.

Behind a gritstone wall, a young farmer tries to chase a cow into his trailer. The cow is skittish. The farmer widens his stance, opening his arms and shouting as the cow bolts up the field. The rest of the herd stands by, warily watching this battle of wills.

Through the trees, the rocks beckon and we keep moving.

———

A couple of years have passed since I last climbed on grit-stone. This is the rock that I first climbed on during my undergraduate years at Liverpool University.

Some climbers can tell you of their first climb with precise detail. Ask, and they will entertain you with a well-rehearsed anecdote of fear and thrills, foolishness and joy. In the legendary climber Joe Brown's autobiography, he describes clambering up the rocks behind the waterfall at Kinder Downfall and later returning to repeat the route with his mother's washing line.[1] Gwen Moffatt started on the Idwal Slabs in Snowdonia when the rocks were frozen and the icy descent proved treacherous enough to require ice axes and abseils.[2] Chris Bonington was shown the ropes at Harrison's Rocks near Tunbridge Wells by his auntie's lodger's assistant, who just happened to be called Cliff.[3]

I can't give you such a story. I struggle to remember my early outdoor climbs on gritstone crags around the Peak District. Where did I go and what did I climb? Froggatt, Stanage, Curbar, the Roaches – such names ring a bell – but I couldn't tell you with any certainty where I went and what routes I climbed. The stony edges have blurred together. Some had trees growing right up around the base of the crag and others looked out across great plains of sweeping bracken and topped out onto a bleak expanse of heather moorland. The wooded crags seemed sheltered and approachable; climbing on the open moorland could feel disconcertingly exposed.

Those early gritstone climbs were a heady fuse of fear and excitement. Hanging around those rocky edges, waiting to get on, I huddled inside my coat, growing cold and tense – and yet as soon as I moved onto the rock, my palms turned hot and sweaty.

Fumbling up routes, following more experienced leaders, I struggled with the moves. I didn't know how to handle the rock or myself in relation to it. I gripped too tight and reached too far, overstretching and pulling myself off balance. When hauling up onto high ledges, I used the most obvious body part – a knee – which was always met with a shout from above or below. Apparently that was bad form.

Falling off, I dangled on the rope, shouting for directions from my partner, who took my weight and leaned over the top, trying to offer some kind of guidance. Later, I returned to my student homes feeling hungry, sore and tired. When the chalk and moorland grime washed away in the shower, I found stinging patches of flesh. Scraped elbows, bruised knees and shins or sunburned shoulders. Climbing always left its mark.

—

At the foot of the crag we prepare for the climb. Unloading our bags, we pull out a mass of equipment. We step into harnesses, pulling them tight at the waist. The ropes are flaked into two neat piles and we tie in to opposite ends. Trainers come off, replaced with tight-fitting rubber-soled climbing shoes. Adam starts to pick through a mass of metal and fabric devices, clipping individual pieces of gear onto loops on his harness. We are traditional climbers, which means that we climb routes without pre-placed safety protection. To safely ascend the rock face, we take a set of gear up with us and hunt out natural openings while we climb, relying on our own gear placements to catch us, should we fall. When we reach the top we build anchor systems, wrapping slings and ropes around blocks, trees and boulders in order to secure each other's passage up the rock face.

Hen Cloud is glittering in the sunshine but I put my fleece back on, remembering the peculiar weather systems that come into play on these exposed edges. Warm and sheltered one moment – the next a cloud comes, the breeze picks up and you find yourself frozen to the rock. These Pennine edges catch the wind, heightening the blast of air towards the top, where you sometimes sit, braced and battered against the localised hurricane.

Adam will lead the first route, which is called Modern. The rule of climbing nomenclature is that the first to climb a route earns the right of naming. The details – route name, date of first ascent and names of ascensionists – are then faithfully recorded in guidebooks, which means that every climb is presented with a precise historical context. Modern is rather unusual in this regard. The guidebook only offers a vague impression – that the route was first climbed sometime between 1947 and 1951 and by unknown climbers. Modern by name; Modernist by nature.

Adam climbs and I pay the rope out, watching his progress, anticipation and tension building inside me. I am eager to get on the rock but I must be patient. Traditional climbing takes time.

Finally, the ropes tighten at my waist and the call comes from above.

'On belay. Climb when ready!'

'Climbing!'

Placing my hands on the stone, I step up into the corner.

My left toes nudge into a scoop and sits tight. My right foot though . . . there's nothing for it. I look closer, examining the surfaces around me. There's a ramp at a steep 40° angle. Should I place my foot on there? There are no distinct kinks or blemishes on the ramp, nothing that would obviously hold my foot in place – just the gritty surface. I widen my search, scanning the rock again, hoping to find something more positive, a definitive feature that declares itself to be 'the hold'. There is nothing.

Many people, when they think of climbing, think of holds and a thing to grasp. That concept does not serve you well on gritstone. It has a rough surface that scrapes at the skin, clawing at knuckles, tearing holes that bleed and smart. But this rough surface is what you must trust. In lieu of holds, you must give yourself to the rock. Trust friction.

I put my right foot onto the ramp, grimacing slightly and tentatively pushing down. My toes stick and I step up, trying to trust my feet while my palms scan the surface for the next hold.

As I reach about, my fingers hunt for an edge, a gap, a crack or a crevice – something, anything to grasp.

There's nothing.

I give up on trying to find a hold and instead open my hands wide and cup the rock, taking huge handfuls of stone as I push down and move my feet up onto a blank shining sandpaper wall.

I climb up to a crack which opens into a wide, round smile and reach for the edges – but there are no edges. The crack curves around onto the face like the roll of a wave. I try to clamp my hand around it, pressing the rough-textured wave into my palm, fingers pushing into the stone, but the edge is too round and wide to grasp.

This is a classic gritstone trick. From the ground, the crack looked promising. It was a defined feature that I thought I would comfortably wrap my hands around. Yet here I am and the rock is pushing back. Hard. Uncompromising.

I shift my hands, my feet, my hips, my weight. Nothing is comfortable. I try one stance and then another; I try one way of holding the rock and then another. It all feels wrong. But there must be some way to do this move. Hidden somewhere, there is a key. This is where a particular technique comes into play.

I should jam.

Ball your hand into a fist and imagine slotting it into a crack in the rock. Twist your wrist and push your fingers out so that your hand expands wide enough to be wedged in tight. Your hand shouldn't move. This is a hand jam, a fundamental technique for gritstone crack climbing.

Pull back on your fist and push yourself up. Feet follow hands. Place a foot in the crack with your knee twisted out, and then turn that leg like a key in a lock so that your knee moves upright and your foot sits secure. Step up. Repeat.

That's the theory.

I ball my hand and sink the fist into the crack. The rock is cool and indifferent. I twist my wrist until the gritstone holds tight. The grit sharpens; its teeth poised, ready to bite. Images of bloodied knuckles and mangled fingers dance before me.

Is the jam too tight? Could my hand get stuck? I try loosening the jam, shifting my wrist and making my fist a little smaller. It doesn't feel right.

Nothing feels right.

I can't jam.

Forgoing dignity, style and technique, I settle for another

approach. Brute force. Grit the teeth and haul. Seizing at whatever my hands can find – a dimple, a chickpea of quartz – I drag my way up and flop over the top to greet Adam.

'How was that?'

'Bloody gritstone.'

He grins, knowingly.

———

Each rock type speaks its own language, which is shaped, in part, by its geology. Different stones are composed of distinctive minerals, giving rise to particular textures and densities of rock which erode in their own characteristic style. Climbers home in on this superficial matter, their focus drawn to the surface, the meeting place of weather and geology. Rocks have patterns, and climbers learn to read these patterns by mapping their body to the stone. In time, all the playful practise of exploration and experimentation builds up into a vocabulary and then you become fluent in the rock.

Some rocks are easier to read than others. There are some that you get on and take to immediately, finding a ready flow of comprehension. Others are more difficult. Some have a complex grammar that you struggle to get your head around and as you make your way into that alien language, you meet frequent stumbling blocks.

Gritstone has an air of simplicity. Unlike rhyolite and limestone – which can weather into a mosaic of holds and fissures – gritstone is not cluttered with excessive detail. It is typically laid out in rounded breaks, cracks, smooth walls and sculpted forms. The routes tend to be short – many a mere ten or twenty metres – and scanning these simple-looking lines, you predict a sequence of moves, anticipate the challenges and set off.

On the rock, however, you discover your mistakes. Sections that looked blank contain hidden gems and the passages that you thought you would sail through suddenly push, prod and harass you. Incompetence is soon laid bare. This is a rock that demands skill.

I am not a native gritstone speaker. I come from a region underscored by Silurian mudstone, a rock that is loose and porous, prone to crumble and shatter. There were no cliffs to play on. Quarried pits appeared here and there, in the oak woods where the stone had been taken out to build a nearby house or barn, but those tumbledown brambled holes offered little worth climbing. In that rolling landscape of hills, woodland, pheasants, farmers and sheep, there were no proper climbers. We scaled trees and scrambled over gates or barbed-wire fences. That was as far as it went.

Gritstone was the first rock that I properly climbed on, but it did not ignite my passion for climbing. Like so many modern climbers, that began indoors, in the urban environment. Moving away from home to study in Liverpool, some new outdoorsy friends took me down the dock roads to an old church. Inside, the pews had gone and there was no font or altar – the towering walls had been repurposed for a different observance. We warmed up in the crypt, clinging to coloured plastic-resin holds, traversing around the room, ducking our heads for the low ceiling. Then we headed up into the nave, where vast lines stretched right up to the rafters.

When I first reached the top, my heart pounded. The

ground was miles away. What was I doing up here? How would I get down? The action of reaching and stretching between the coloured holds to pull myself up the wall was so absorbing that I hadn't noticed how high I had climbed until suddenly I ran out of holds and was at the top, cheeks glowing with triumph while my stomach swooped.

With repeat trips up to the rafters, I soon forgot the height and began to find rhythm, sequence, coordination and power. I discovered that good climbing flowed. Climbing was dancing and it left a very real impression upon the body. For days afterwards, I felt the strain in my arms, shoulders, legs and stomach. Such aches were oddly pleasurable. The pain that came after a good session – all of those deep-muscle aches and twinges, the struggle to raise a glass or put on a coat – taught me about my physique. On the wall I became a network of muscles, limbs, senses, nerves, cells and neurons; an active, thinking, sensing being. Indoor climbing giving me a new map of my body. Forget body image – this was body physical.

———

After following Adam up Modern, it is my turn to lead. I take the gear from his harness and we move around to Central Crack. Unlike Modern, this classic has a well-rehearsed origin story. In 1909 John Laycock pioneered the route, but his second, A.R. Thomson, struggled to follow him up, which resulted in Laycock almost being stranded on the cliff overnight – an impressive feat for a forty-metre rock face. Fortunately a sturdy chauffeur turned up and rescued him.

Stepping onto the rock, my foot slips straight back off again. The route has gone the way of many old classics. Since Laycock's time, thousands of people have been up here, each one leaving their own minute impression upon the grit, collectively wearing the footholds clean until they are polished pink and smooth as soapstone. This is not the first time that I have had to fight to get off the ground. Many easy gritstone routes have near impenetrable starts because the all-essential friction has worn away.

Finding rock with more texture, I push up into a large, dark crack where the rock steepens and the crack pushes back. No matter how I arrange my hands and feet, I can't shake the feeling that the grit is trying to push me off.

In past years, this is where I would have started cursing. Profusely.

Instead, I try laybacking the crack; wrapping my right hand around the sloping edge and walking my feet up the wall. My forearms swell, hardening like concrete.

And once again there are no positive footholds – just the gritty face to push against. The move is hard. I back off and climb down to a more comfortable stance. I breathe and shake my limbs out.

'You had it there. Go on, you can do it!'

Adam's encouragement helps.

On the third attempt, I push up and place my left foot high on a wrinkle in the gritstone, ignoring my misgivings. Pressing down on the toes, I stand up, gasping. I've done the move – but the rock doesn't let up. The gritstone is still pushing back, jabbing at my chest, legs and feet, leaving me off-balance and fighting to stay on.

The crack widens. There are still no holds but I spot an

opening. I thrust my hips into the crack and wedge myself in tight, facing outwards to occupy this natural vantage point like the Antony Gormley statue half-buried in the sands north of Liverpool. I have just mastered the hip-jam.

Below us, walkers trudge up the path, chattering and laughing through waist-high bracken. They pause, hands shading their eyes as they squint up, watching our progress on the crags. For a moment, our worlds meet and we stand together – fellow outdoor enthusiasts sharing a sunny Saturday morning in the Peak District. Then they pick up their feet and move on with ease and I remember where I am. Halfway up a gritstone edge, facing yet another improbably blank-looking ramp.

When I finally complete the pitch and Adam joins me, grimacing on the ledge, he affirms my struggle.

'That was slippy as a bastard.'

The drama of gritstone can only really be appreciated first-hand.

Many climbers cut their teeth on gritstone. The moorland outcrops that line the high tops of Staffordshire, Cheshire, Derbyshire and Yorkshire are accessible to huge numbers of people. The Peak District National Park, which encompasses many of these popular Pennine gritstones, is one of the most visited national parks in the UK. Surrounded by the old northern industrial towns and cities of Manchester, Sheffield, Leeds, Stoke-on-Trent and Nottingham, some 20 million people live within an hour's journey of the park and 50 million live within four hours of this essential elevated green space.

Unsurprisingly, the crags are rarely quiet. Locals and visitors alike flock to the rocks at evenings and weekends all year round. Even in winter, climbers will get stuck into the stony edges. Friction improves in the cold. While some tuck into turkey dinners and others go for a bracing dip, every 25 December a devoted throng takes to Christmas Crack on Stanage. Among the down jackets, waterproofs, mince pies and thermos flasks, expect to see Santa hats and reindeer onesies.

The gritstone edges might not have the dramatic stature of a mountain crag, but they have their own grand scale of opportunity, which is best showcased by Stanage, a two-mile-long outcrop overlooking Hathersage, Bamford and the Hope Valley. That great moorland edge of umpteen exposed blocks, corners and faces holds nearly 2,000 climbs. There are easy slabs and brutally blank walls as well as a plethora of green chimneys for the troglodytes to get stuck into. A climber can lose themselves inside runnels, alcoves and cave-like features or hang out, exposed, on wind-blasted arêtes. On the quarried faces you can try out the more angular lines, mantling onto breaks and ledges, pausing to look out over the piles of discarded millstones, the work of previous generations of rock men, now fading into the bracken.

The rocks that provide all this excitement, keeping so many people occupied in the present moment, were formed some 320 million years ago, when Britain lay at the equator. In the tropical climate of the Carboniferous period, lush forests of giant club mosses, tree ferns and great horsetails flourished. This plant matter slowly decayed into peat, which in time was compressed, hardening into dense black carbon, giving us our coal measures. Then, the Pennines were not an upland spine – the Pennine Basin was a space into which rivers drained from Himalayan-scale mountains. Like the Ganges Delta today, this was the place where the river flow slowed, the waters fanning out into vast deltas depositing sediments. The silt, sand and gravel built up in layers that hardened into the rock now known as Millstone Grit or gritstone. Place your hands on the gritstone, and you are plunging your fingers into ancient riverbeds and sandbanks.

——

Checking my watch, I see, with the usual jolt, that the morning has gone. Time does strange things on the rock. Minutes expand – hours vanish.

We settle for lunch on grassy ledges below the crag, negotiating a quick trade (half of my banana for one of Adam's chocolate bars), and I relax, letting my eyes wander. Staffordshire stretches out in a soft, rolling green carpet of grass, bracken, hedgerows and woodland. In a few weeks, the colours will turn and this prospect will be transformed into a great autumnal display, but not just yet. The reservoir shines in the sunlight and even further out the land fades into the blue haze of the Cheshire plain.

A trio of climbers arrive, eyeing up Central Crack.

'How was it?' one of them asks.

I roll my eyes and offer a few choice comments on the particularities of gritstone.

The leader grins. He has also travelled down from Scotland and shares my gritstone affliction.

While he struggles on the first few moves, we finish lunch, repack our bags and head on. Adam is working his way through the Classic Rock ticklist and has two routes to complete at the Roaches. To endure the struggles, pains and frustrations of climbing, it can help to be reasonably goal-oriented. Many climbers have desire lists that they are working their way through, ticking off routes to check their progress. Classic Rock is one such list. Like the Munros – a set of mountains over 3,000 feet in Scotland – or the Wainwright hills in the Lake District, the Classic Rock list has many aspirants. The list, featuring eighty-three of the best 'easy' climbs across the UK, is compiled from a book of illustrated essays put together by Ken Wilson in 1978. As well as accessible crags like the Roaches, *Classic Rock* contains routes on sea cliffs, islands and remote mountains, bringing a marked element of adventure to the undertaking. The black and white photographs of soaring rock lines make for excellent dreaming on winter nights and wet weekends.

Circling the base of Hen Cloud, we head up onto the moor where the colour palette shifts from green to yellows and browns. We have entered the world of peat, heather and pale grasses. *Getback-getback-getback.* A grouse takes flight. Long grass whips in the wind. Black outcrops break up the moorland. Staring into the wind, I look down on fields, farms and woodland. Turning my back, I gaze out across a vast, rolling heather sea full of light and depth. Some say that moorland is bleak, but up here, I always feel a little closer to the sky.

This is one of the things I love about gritstone climbing: the sense of climbing from one world to another, again and again. I love topping out. It is easy to forget, when you are turned into the rock and every inch of you is absorbed with the ascent, that you are climbing towards a natural vantage point. Once anchored to a boulder or two at the top and settled on the edge beside some rain-weathered bowl, toes dangling over the precipice; then, after the strain of intense physical focus on vertical stony details, the horizontal plane can become a startling opening. Eyes wander, starting to roam out, and the body decompresses, finally gaining the relief of space.

Today the moor is busy. Relaxed walkers and red-faced runners in fluorescent T-shirts jostle along the path. The Roaches is buzzing. People lie out in the sun, texting, laughing and chatting. Music plays. Walkers, dogs and climbers weave between rocks, bags and bodies.

'Hasn't he done well?' A proud father invites us to praise his teenage son. 'This is the first time he's ever climbed outside!' The boy, wearing army combat trousers, smiles despite himself.

Another father tries to persuade his teenage daughter to keep climbing. She folds her arms inside her oversized hoodie and scowls. She has had enough.

A young crew traipses through the crowds, each clad in vest and sunglasses with hefty colourful crash mats strapped to their backs. They reach a boulder and the mats come down, opening out like butterflies to be laid flat on the ground, forming a padded circle around the stone. One of the crew changes her shoes and dips her hands into a fabric bucket of white chalk before running her fingers over the rock; eventually they settle upon a couple of chalk-whitened chinks. Toes slide into a slot and she is on, braced to begin the problem. The friends cluster in, forming a supportive ring, arms held aloft ready to guide her body, should she fall, onto the mats, but she is strong and slaps up for the next move while her comrades shout positive affirmations.

Bouldering – the practice of climbing short problems on low rocks which do not require the use of ropes and harnesses – has always been part of the climbing repertoire, but in recent years it has exploded in popularity. The small routes don't look much, but they have led to a transformation in the climbing community.

Back in the early 2000s, it was not uncommon for a woman visiting an indoor climbing wall to be the only woman in that space. Now, indoor walls are full of girls and women. Sometimes I go in and marvel at the change. It seems like a quiet revolution has happened in the last ten years. Now, increasing numbers of climbing gyms are approaching a fifty-fifty male–female membership. The change is a little slower in the outdoors, but nonetheless, it is happening there too. In just a few years, the climbing community has come to look and feel very different.

The catalyst for this dramatic diversification was the birth of the indoor bouldering wall. In these warm, welcoming spaces, there are no ropes, harnesses or towering lead walls. The routes go no higher than two metres. A climber simply puts on a pair of shoes, grabs the holds and has a go, dropping back down safely onto the mats below when they are done. Bouldering walls remove many barriers, letting people get stuck straight into the pleasures of movement and embodied problem-solving.

When the first gym of this kind opened in Sheffield in 2006, the manager was told it would never work. Now the model pioneered at Climbing Works is repeated in urban centres across the world. From Hereford to San Francisco,

Hull to Paris and Tokyo, bouldering walls are springing up everywhere and when they open, a host of eager new climbers burst in through the doors. While indoor bouldering is fun and accessible, don't be fooled into thinking that it's easy. What the bouldering route lacks in stature, it more than makes up for in challenge. Boulderers typically practise much harder moves than one meets on a traditional climb. The pursuit centres on short, sharp problems that require huge strength, power and dexterity to solve. When you finally find the key to unlock the sequence of moves that has troubled you for some time – perhaps nailing the flow by adding in a toe hook and a certain tilt of the hip – the satisfaction far exceeds the scale of the ascent.

—

Our next route takes us onto Black and Tans, which begins beside a leaning pillar of rock at the base of a sizeable buttress. Sliding in to start behind a holly tree, I find the ledges have been worn red-raw with the passage of many hands and feet, but I move comfortably, swinging around the arête to emerge onto an open slab. This face is lined with delicate edges, leading into a corner where I balance up the groove, pushing against the sides, slotting into the well-used holds as the ground retreats below me in an easy height gain. Moving with the rock, the piece handles with fluid ease.

Unlike Hen Cloud, where the angled rock seemed determined to push me off at every turn, this buttress feels much more accommodating. My fingers slide over the polished surfaces – gently pressing down on the smooth ledges – with no fearful clamping. The rougher textures press up into the skin, melding into the contours of my fingertips, creating a close, warm contact.

The following route is similarly relaxing. I scale Technical Slab slowly, leaning into the grooves and openings, enjoying the sensation of pressing my feet onto the grit, padding up the wall and running my palms over the pebble bumps, letting the rock do the work of holding me in place. Flowing up the sunlit stone, I soak up the afternoon ambience and a haze of tranquillity starts to settle over me.

Down at the Lower Tier, we stop to examine one last route. This one has a more commanding presence. It has been on my radar for a while – a desire line that ignites a certain flicker of excitement and intimidation. The route heads up a steep green corner and then moves left, traversing across the middle of the rock face, dropping down a great nose-shaped flake of orange rock before stepping out left to finish up the arête, hanging out over an abyss of open air.

Peering up into those shapely features, my palms prickle and stomach flutters. I study the crux, a sequence of exposed moves that will lead me out into a moment of critical balance, poised across the void on two points of friction.

Valkyrie looks brilliant.

But I'm not in the zone. My fight has gone, left behind somewhere in the cracks of Hen Cloud. Right now my arms and legs feel heavy and my thoughts are drifting off the moor, heading down towards the woozy sunshine of a beer garden.

'Tomorrow.'

———

The next morning we diligently pack our bags for another day on the rock, but things have changed.

The crags have vanished. An autumnal mist has crept in and the cloud is clamping down on the landscape in a smothering lid that sits so low that even the fields have disappeared behind the damp stone walls. Cows loom through the murk, glimpsed as lumbering beasts with steam pouring from their nostrils. In the gorse bushes, light radiates from water droplets suspended on spider threads.

Despite the weather, we traipse back up to the Roaches, cherishing a vague hope that perhaps the rock will be dry and we will find something to climb. Drizzle speckles the waterproof jacket that I begged from a friend this morning.

We reach the crags, and the tops are lost in cloud. There is no music this morning. No mats or bags. No one else is here. The party is over. We wander along the base of the crag, assessing the damp rock.

I try a low-level traverse, swinging from huge round holds, keeping my feet on the rock face. Pausing to hang from one arm, I stop to dry my wet fingers on my trousers. Lines of water run down the rock, glistening silver in the morning light.

Then we hear the clang of metal and, like Pavlov's dogs, the sound stirs a conditioned response. We rush over, gravitating towards the noise, curious to see what the other climbers have found. Hoods up, shoulders hunched, they are wrapped tight in waterproofs with their rope trailing in a pool of water. We are not inspired.

Valkyrie will have to wait.

We drop back down to the valley, our feet sliding in mud and slipping on the sodden stones as we pass hordes of grim-faced climbers trudging up to survey the scene for themselves.

—

Returning to climb in the Peak District now, I am struck by how sociable these exposed moorland edges are. Parents, children, instructors, novices, climbing clubs, university groups and world-class climbers can all be found here, working side by side, each occupied with their own problems. The Carboniferous gritstones are now some of the most touched rocks in Britain. They lie at the heart of the outdoor climbing community.

Such lively informal outdoor gatherings put me in mind of the seaside. A trip to the crags is as much of an occasion as a trip to the beach. Both places draw people from all walks of life; deliberately choosing that spot to linger, take time out and be somewhere else. In both spaces, people instinctively become immersed – wandering, exploring, probing, playing, relaxing – losing themselves in their immediate environment. But just 100 years ago, the pleasure and fulfilment that so many of us find in the Peak District would have been unthinkable.

Private property.

Keep out.

No trespassing.

Access to the countryside was the preserve of the wealthy elite. To visit the Peak you had to be canny. Angry farmers and violent gamekeepers were all too ready to catch and forcibly remove trespassers. At Stanage, climbers were said to have bribed the gamekeeper with barrels of beer, and at

Windgather, in the 1940s, Joe Brown and his mates kept a sharp eye out for the farmer who guarded the rocky fortress like a medieval villain, chipping off holds and pouring tar over popular sections of the crag.[4] Getting outside required a rebellious spirit; a determination to disobey the law of gates, fences, signs and possessive landowners.

Things changed with the outdoors movement. From the start of the twentieth century, growing numbers of urban workers began to access the countryside at the weekend. We weren't supposed to be on the moors, but still, we went. Cycling, climbing, camping, caravanning and youth hostelling were some of the chosen activities of this surging movement; but above all, rambling – a little like the indoor climbing movement of today – was the real craze. Walking, which seems so banal to many modern climbers, was a radical act of physical, political and philosophical transgression. Tensions mounted.

A defining moment came on 24 April 1932, when 400 people took to Kinder Scout for a mass trespass, organised by the British Worker's Sports Federation with members from the Young Communist League. The activist ramblers met in Bowden Quarry and listened to speeches, before heading up William Clough, where they wrestled through a pack of gamekeepers and climbed victoriously up onto the moor. At Ashop Head they met another crew of rambler-trespasser comrades who had come over from Sheffield: meeting thus, the two groups declared the trespass a success. Afterwards, five people were arrested, tried and jailed. The harsh sentencing, which aimed to dissuade further ramblers, sparked outrage and the movement grew. Two months later, a rally at Winnat's Pass drew 10,000 people.

Land is power; but there is also power in numbers. With such popular demand, the government's hand was forced. In the years that followed a spate of Acts came in: the Rights of Way Act (1932), Access to the Mountains Act (1939) and National Parks and Access to the Countryside Act (1949), bringing greater rights, access and freedom for all. In 1951, the Peak District became the first national park in the UK.

—

In June 2020, just after the first round of Covid restrictions relaxed, I headed into the Peak once again, making for Stanage where I met my friend Helen beside the Dennis Knoll plantation. Walking in through light drizzle, we passed a heap of abandoned millstones, now lichened and disappearing into the bracken. Ahead rose the great slabs, blocks and cracks of High Neb.

The grit was damp but we climbed anyway, both delighted to be out again, easing our way back into the practice. I had not climbed for months, but like riding a bike, everything came flooding back. Ropes, gear, harness, guidebook: it was good to handle that equipment once again; to feel the familiar pull of the rope; to hear the jangle of the nuts, hexes, quickdraws and cams. For Helen it was also a big moment. On Tango Crack and Mantleshelf Climb, she led her first routes since having a baby.

On Kelly's Variation, I grappled around for a while, hesitant about committing to a delicate move inside a damp groove. The step felt risky. I would need to smear on wet grit – pressing the sole of my rubber shoes onto the slab and using friction to gain ground – with my hands clasping nothing of significance. I felt around, rearranging my hands and feet, trying this stance and that, experimenting with any number of combinations, but there was no great revelation. It seemed there was only one way to do it.

Trusting the technique, I went for it – stepping up onto the damp smear and reaching as I moved – and the gritstone provided. With the height gain, my hand slid over the ledge and found – oh – completely hidden from view, a water-worn bowl. Clasping the defined rim, I pulled up with confidence, laughing onto the ledge.

II

YORKSHIRE

GRITSTONE

The country grows into the image of the people and the people grow into the likeness of the country until, to the soul's geographer, each becomes a symbol of the other.
– The Wheels of the World, *RTÉ, 1974*[5]

Fingers cling to a nick in the rock; below, my toes are thrust into another tiny opening. My body screams with the tension: forearms and calves burn hot and hard. I take my right hand off and reach up to place my fingers into another slot, pinching tight. The strain increases. I long for a rest, to find a comfortable stance where I can relax my focus and let my muscles breathe.

But this is Yorkshire gritstone. The face is blank apart from the steep line of chipped holds onto which I desperately cling. There is no point searching for alternatives. The route is like a ladder, except there are no rungs: just minuscule cuts in the rock. I am climbing Cow Udder, a route on the flank of a towering rock face known as the Cow. At my back, somewhere away, below, out of sight and far from mind, sits her offspring – the Calf; a megalithic boulder that was torn free during the time of ice.

My right foot slips from its enclave and for a moment my

leg swings loose. Fingers clench tight – an instinctive pinch – and my hips move back into the rock. I regain balance. Focus. I put the foot back on, this time pushing the toes further inside the nook, finding a few more precious millimetres. Breathe. I can do this. Head down, grip, keep moving.

Perhaps the route got its name because each hold is no bigger than a cow's teat; or maybe because each move is like squeezing a drop of milk from a dry udder.

'Hurry up,' my partner calls from the top.

My temperature surges. Why is he rushing me? Climbing takes time; this is a difficult route.

I throw curses up the wall at him and carry on, trying to recover my poise.

'Come on!'

My rage increases. What is his problem?

With each move, I feel the rope tighten at my waist, impelling me upwards. He is belaying with urgency, charging the line with a forceful current. The rope takes over; I am losing the rock. What is going on?

I reach the top, pull up over the gritstone edge and emerge to a different world. The sky is black. From the shelter of the warm rock, I had not seen the impending storm. Now I'm facing apocalypse on the edge of Ilkley Moor. The Wharfe valley is disappearing under immense clouds. Curtains of rain move in. The air turns cold; a drop lands on my cheek. A sudden flash and everything is illuminated; moments later a deep rumble shakes my frame. I catch myself: we are the tallest figures on a huge, rolling moor, and we have an arsenal of metal clipped to our waists. We have to move.

'Quick!'

We frantically dismantle the anchors and coil the rope then scarper, leaping across gritstone blocks, mindful of cracks and holes as we scurry down the steep sandy banks, back into the quarry. A strange darkness descends. The picnic benches are empty. Huge raindrops burst on the dust – but we reach the car and slam the doors. Rain hammers the roof as the storm moves overheard. Lightning tears the dark sky apart.

—

My climbing cranked up a notch in Yorkshire. Moving to Leeds in 2014 to start a PhD, my time was suddenly my own. As long as I met my deadlines it did not matter when or how I worked. No one was watching. The freedom was incredible. I worked hard to get things done so that I could get out as much as possible. Leaving behind the glorious chaos of colour, music, drink and conversation that spilled out of the back-to-back terraces of Leeds, I frequently headed out north and west along the Otley Road to the crags. Almscliff, Caley, Baildon Bank, the Cow and Calf, Rylstone, Brandrith: there were plenty of gritty brown outcrops to keep a climber occupied. Unlike the famous Peak District edges of Stanage, the Roaches and Froggatt, where hundreds of routes are attended by hundreds of climbers, the Wharfedale crags were generally smaller and less busy – although a fine summer evening at Almscliff reliably drew out the crowds. While the rock faces were quiet, we rarely climbed alone. Many people lovingly roamed over God's Own Country, from dog walkers to multi-generational Muslim families and elderly couples armed with anoraks and thermos flasks, all of whom might stop to occupy the benches, taking in the huge views that opened across rolling hills. Sometimes, as the sun set, all of the fields, moorland and wooded valleys briefly burned golden. I soon understood why Yorkshire men and women believe they live in heaven on earth.

The views could be enchanting; the land and people were welcoming; but God's Own rock is hard. In damp weather, the crags lurk in the heather like a bunch of surly trolls. In sunshine, the coarse grit buttresses stand proud, thrusting out their rounded cracks and impenetrable faces, fiercely staring down any would-be adventurers. Yorkshire grit climbing has a particular character, which partly plays off regional stereotypes. Like any good Yorkshireman, a grit climber should be stubborn, determined and tight: ever ready to tussle with the rock and wean out a victory from the meanest of circumstances. After all, climbing in biting winds or driving rain is character-building. For the uninitiated and the experienced alike, a gritstone climb can be a sobering experience. Rumours circle through the climbing community that some routes are 'undergraded', meaning that the climb is much more difficult than the advertised grade would suggest. Falling off a route far below your usual standard provides a hard lesson in humility. At those moments, it is best to have a Yorkshireman on hand. Before you brush off that chastening moment and excuse your failure through bluff and bluster – Bloody gritstone!; the weather was all wrong; who wrote this goddamn guidebook? – with blunt sincerity and a slight smile the Yorkshireman will tell you straight:

'You've gone soft, mate.'

Geologically speaking, there is little difference between Peak District and Yorkshire gritstone. Across the region, the Millstone Grit varies slightly in quality – in places the grain is fine, in other places small pebbles line the rock – but essentially the grit is all old river debris that was deposited in the Pennine Basin some 320 million years ago. Along with the Dark Peak, the rolling hills and moorland of West Yorkshire form part of the Pennines – the upland spine of northern England. Similarly, in the climbing world, little difference is drawn between Peak District and Yorkshire grit. Instead, to the Yorkshire climber, Lancashire is the antagonist. The clash between the houses of York and Lancaster during the Wars of the Roses might seem like distant history learned in hazily remembered classrooms for many people, but in certain places the feud lives on, although now the conflict is fought through humour rather than military action. Barbs are hidden inside the *Yorkshire Gritstone* climbing guidebook. Widdop, a crag right on the contentious county border, contains detailed access notes for those coming from Hebden Bridge (in Yorkshire), after which follows a brief statement for the Lancastrians:

> If approaching from Lancashire, you have our sympathies, but rumour has it that tarmacadam actually winds its way up from Nelson and Burnley to Widdop reservoir.[6]

Yorkshire gritstone is a rock inscribed with character. On this rough brown stone, regional identity is found and performed, time and time again.

———

On Yorkshire grit, I tried out the terrifying business of lead climbing once again. Unlike seconding, where you are generally safe because you always have a rope above you, leading is much more risky. You must protect yourself as you go by connecting the rope to the rock as you climb. Then, if you fall, you plummet down onto the nearest piece of protection, which ideally will hold your weight when the rope pulls tight.

There are two ways of protecting a lead climb. One requires you to carry up an arsenal of metal and reinforced-fabric devices that you must skilfully slot into cracks as you go; once you have safely completed the route, your partner will follow you up, removing these precious pieces of metalware. This is known as traditional climbing. The other way is to clip your rope onto a set of bolts that have been drilled into the rock and will remain fixed in place for someone else to use after you have gone. This is sport climbing. Generally speaking, sport climbing is safer and more straightforward than traditional climbing. As you might expect, Yorkshire gritstone is a bastion of traditional climbing.

Sport climbing took off in the 1980s with the advent of the cordless drill. Before this, bolting the rock was labour intensive, reliant on either a hand drill (which took a lot of time) or an electric drill powered by a long cable and generator. When the cordless drill hit the climbing scene (often used in combination with homemade 'turbo' battery packs, since early batteries had short lifespans), things rapidly changed. Crags and quarries rang with the sound of drills and hammers, as climbers hung from the rock faces, adding fixed points of protection to routes. Suddenly traditional routes that were desperately challenging and dangerous became much more accessible. With fixed protection on the rock face, a climber no longer faced such a heady dice with death. Steep and blank faces became safer. Sport climbing eliminates exposed runouts – long distances between points of protection – and reduces the potential for gear failure. When you fall on a bolt, the rope catches with a stern jolt. When you fall on a piece of metal that you slotted into the rock face yourself moments before, there can be some doubt. The piece might hold; it might not. As you plummet and your weight loads onto the metal, the piece may slip – wedging in deeper – or it may rip out and your fall will continue down, landing you with greater force onto the next piece below. This is why it's important to learn to place good gear.

The advent of sport climbing was a highly contentious moment. Divisions emerged and disputes erupted. Routes were bolted and bolts were cut and then climbs were re-bolted and re-cut again. Members of the climbing community bickered and fought in open hostilities that were more heated than any recent disputes along the Lancashire–Yorkshire border.

The problem was a clash in values. With improved safety, sport climbers could focus on physical challenges, developing the gymnastics of the sport. On bolted routes, movement, strength and agility are paramount. But this, argued the traditionalists, was not proper climbing. Keeping your cool on exposed faces; climbing into the unknown; learning the craft of gear placement: as well as physical strength and technique, traditional climbing places significant demands on the mind. This is what's known as the all-important 'head game'.

Leave the rock as you find it. Reduce injuries and death. Increase accessibility. Maintain challenge. The aesthetics and ethics of the dispute raged on. However, when I came to Yorkshire grit, the dispute had been settled, in this region at least. My battered 1998 guidebook unequivocally set out the result:

> Bolts should not play any part in modern gritstone climbing, and apart from one obvious and rather embarrassing exception at Caley, have all but been eradicated and should never be re-placed.[7]

———

In my early climbing days in the Peak District, I had had a few abortive attempts at traditional leading – I even made it up a few routes. But generally, if the rope and gear were offered to me, I recoiled, backing off in the same way that one might if a zookeeper offered a tiger on a leash and asked you to take it for a walk. Leading was terrifying; the risks manifold. But in Yorkshire, I came to the rock with a new thirst for adventure. After years of indoor climbing, I had reached a certain level of technical ability. Inside those warm, safe, sociable spaces, I had found so much pleasure navigating the walls and solving the colourful problems. Now I wanted to expand my craft. I wanted to climb, outside, at the sharp end of the rope, leading my own routes. One fine spring day, I walked into Hetchell Woods, armed with gear, rope and guidebook. I was intent on getting a lead climb in.

From the car park, I picked my way through the muddy trails, squelching and sliding along beside my partner, Will.

Like me, he was a trad-climbing novice in his mid-twenties. We had met in the bouldering gyms of Leeds, where we worked at climbing problems together – figuring out moves, falling off, trying again – laughing and flirting in the thick chalky air. In those old industrial buildings, attraction and trust had built between us and a shared ambition was formed. Neither of us had climbed much outside, but together, we committed to the challenge. We wanted to become trad climbers.

We wandered on and I lapped up my surroundings. There were hazel thickets and jays squawking, ash trees and chattering magpies, the tinkle of a small beck and flushes of wild garlic. The environment felt delightfully familiar. While I had never been to Hetchell before, I had grown up poking around similar muddy dells – clambering trees, wading through ditches and falling into nettle patches. Hazelnuts, adders, hedgehogs, ladybirds, flints, feathers and birds' nests – there was always so much to discover. In these lively, cluttered, intimate woodland spaces, crunching over dead leaves and rotten branches, I felt at home. Within the woods at Hetchell, I sensed that perhaps rock climbing could be something different than I had previously considered. Rather than a serious, professional sport where you tested your limits and diced with death, perhaps it could be a continuation of my beloved childhood forays. Perhaps spending time on rock would bring new ways of relating to the natural environment.

Beyond the beech trees, we came out into the oaks, where tiny patches of colour beckoned from between small green-leaved tufts. The violets were out. Soon the bluebells would come. The canopy opened and the crag emerged. Light flickered across the rock, shadows drawing out the breaks, cracks and ledges. Like many sandstone crags, the layers were obvious. Distinct bands showed where river debris had piled up and hardened in different stages. Strange to think that all this matter had once washed off a mountain, perhaps, and then sat deep underground and under sea, ossifying over aeons. Now it stood exposed to the elements, the surface gradually eroding and dissolving away, particle by particle. The rock cycle is so much slower than the water cycle and thus harder to comprehend, but the results can be spectacular. In Hetchell, the sandy scarp sat in the middle of the woods like a forgotten relic from some ancient civilisation.

Ditching our bags at a dead tree trunk, we began to sort out the climbing kit. I would lead Pompeii Chimney. If the route had been bolted I would only have needed to carry a few lightweight quickdraws, but by the time we were finished piling gear onto my harness, a great range of metalware dangled from my waist. Nuts, hexes, slings, screwgates and quickdraws jangled and clattered, dragging the harness down into my hips. I tied into the rope, slipped on my climbing shoes and stepped up to the rock.

We were told not to climb here after rain, when water soaked into the stone, loosening the surface. Then the rock was delicate, and climbing could be harmful. But that day it was dry, tough and ready to meet our embrace.

The first few moves were straightforward enough. I reached and pulled, bringing my feet up and away from the ground, hands soon getting the feel for the sandy rock, body pushing off ledges. The gear tugged at my waist. All that clunking metal was heavy – weighing perhaps as much as three or four bags of sugar. Gravity liked this load – the further I climbed, the more the ground pulled, seeking to draw me back down into its earthy arms. I resisted, climbing on, looking to offload some metal into the rock.

In the chimney, I spotted a promising crack and wedged myself into the corner, back against the wall, legs taut, pushing down on the edges. Then commenced the awkward scrabble of trying to place some gear. With thorough knowledge of your rack and exceptional coordination, the craft of placing gear is smooth and satisfying. When climbing well, I can look at a crack and know, instinctively, exactly which piece of gear would fit in there.

However, it takes some time to reach such fluidity between hand, eye, metal and rock. In the early days, placing gear was like playing a game of Twister with a particularly sadistic Twister-master. Everything was jumbled, awkward and confusing. Balance was off. Fingers and eyes leaped from crack to harness, to gear, to crack, failing to make much sense of the problem. There were so many different pieces of equipment – how did you know which one was right?

'Try a hex,' Will called up from below.

Hexes. Big, hollow metal hexagons that clang like cowbells. I had four clipped to my harness. The smallest was plumsized and the largest was like a grapefruit.

'The red one.'

Twisting and turning, I leaned around, peering at the devices circling my waist while one hand clung to the wall and the other clattered through the metal, trying to find the hexes. They must be here somewhere.

Aha!

Shaking fingers separated the red hex from the others and began trying to slot it into the rock. The trick was to slide the piece into the wide opening and then pull it down until the crack narrowed and the gear sat tight. Fingers bumped and grazed the rough surface as I worked the piece, wiggling, tugging, testing and adjusting. A chunk of skin left one of my knuckles and a white hole appeared. It would bleed in a minute. Finally, the hex seemed about right. I yanked hard on the fabric loop and it held. I clipped in the rope and shook out my muscles.

—

Flushed with success after I led Pompeii Chimney, we perused the guidebook, looking for another promising line. Many of the climbs at Hetchell have Roman-inspired names. There was Cassius Crawl, When in Rome, The Fall of the Roman Empire and Et Tu Brute. The theme speaks to Pompocali, an archaeological site of distinctive earthworks that lies just beyond the woods' edge. At one time, the mounds at Pompocali were thought to be a Roman fort; now the heaps are considered to be waste material from quarrying. The history may have been updated but the Roman names need not be erased. A Roman road cuts between the woods and earthworks, connecting a fort at Ilkley with settlements in Adel and Calcaria (now known as Tadcaster); the quarrying at Pompocali may have been done by these industrious Romans. Suddenly, through the whims of climbers I had never met, whose own imperial mission led them to create and name many lines across this small gritstone outcrop, I saw a different Yorkshire. The rolling green hills, moorlands and fertile valleys in which I stood became part of a huge European empire. Camps, forts and settlements linked by an extensive road network – their world order, some two thousand years ago, was not so dissimilar from ours. Once I knew to look, the traces of another time and culture overlapped with ours, everywhere. Climbing had conjured a sequence of unexpected cultural connections within the landscape. Yorkshire broadened and deepened.

My next challenge was Centurion.

This time, things did not go so well. Far from embodying the route's namesake on the rock, my lack of skill, strategy and confidence became all too apparent. My performance was not one of a Roman legionary but more of a quaking, shaking rag doll.

The route was more difficult – fewer holds, less protection, steeper angles – and, halfway up, the intense mental strain of leading began to take its toll. Eyes narrowed, flitting across the rock, skittering from one feature to another, struggling to comprehend the whole. There was so little gear. My hands gripped tighter; muscles began to tire. I felt conscious of the gaping distance between the ground and myself, thoughts began racing and legs started shaking.

'I don't know what to do!'

A dreadful tension was building within me.

'Can you reach that ledge?'

Stretching up into wobbling precarity, fingers crawled up onto the ledge, throwing me further out of balance. My last piece of gear was so far below – if I fell here –

'There's no gear – it feels awful!'

'Well . . . have a look?'

'I AM looking!'

Higher up more cracks appeared, maybe I could get something in up there – should I go for it? Adrenaline ripped through me, setting everything pulsing, beating and vibrating. My heart pounded, mouth went dry and legs shook even more violently but still I dragged my body up. From this new stance, quaking hands fumbled through the nuts, trying to slot one into a crack.

The tension grew and grew.

One seemed about right – but then the nuts dropped. Six small pieces of metal rained down onto Will.

'Careful!'

Rag doll turned volcano – a terrible energy was surging and building within – and at that point, I exploded. Fuming, thundering, quaking; swearing, raging, shouting; adult dignity vanished as emotion surged and ruptured. Somehow, I held on and climbed on, hauling up the final moves to flop, panting, over the top.

Cooling off at the top of the crag, I turned self-critical. As well as learning to place gear, I needed to keep a better handle on the stress of leading. I had managed all the moves – the route was well within my physical capability – but leading added a critical extra strain. Feeling insecure and exposed at the sharp end of the rope, a fearful agitation had built up within me, escalating into a desperately heightened pitch. Centurion had taught me a couple of painful lessons. Climbing worked best within a different headspace. Somehow I needed to occupy a cooler, calmer and more composed place on the rock.

———

Beyond the shelter of Hetchell Woods, we spent many exposed hours on wind-blasted moors, freezing on buttresses that seemed at best impenetrable and at worst, openly hostile. Again and again, my climbing trips took me into the heart of Brontë country. Here I found the bleak grouse moorland, treeless heaths and thick-set stone houses of *Jane Eyre* and *Wuthering Heights*. Haworth was close by, that steep stony village where Charlotte, Emily and Anne toiled inside the gritstone parsonage, producing searing works of elemental art. In *Wuthering Heights*, Cathy famously compares her love for Heathcliff to the 'eternal rocks beneath' and on the hard gritstone edges of West Yorkshire, it seemed that the spirit of Heathcliff lived on.[8] Abrupt, rough, sometimes brutally savage and yet strangely compelling, the spirit of the stones uncannily resembled Emily Brontë's arresting villain.

'Rough as a saw-edge, and hard as whinstone! The less you meddle with him the better.'[9] So Mr Lockwood, the newcomer, is warned, and the novel abounds with the troubles that come with meetings with Heathcliff. Clever and alluring, Heathcliff draws people in with invitations that never truly reflect the experience on offer. Characters rarely escape unscathed. So gritstone also pulled me in. Again and again, I went to this rock and, again and again, as I struggled to read and handle its inscrutable character, the experience was fraught and troubling. Yet I knew, somewhere within it all, there was a peculiar savage beauty to the rock. Flailing about on the rough crags, I longed to sing and dance the gritstone with the passion of Kate Bush.

———

Learning to lead on Yorkshire gritstone meant spending many hours inside chimneys, where the easier routes lie.

These louring cracks, wide enough to fit your whole body inside, split the climbing community. They are marmite. Some climbers love chimneys; many hate them. Dark, confined, sometimes wet, green and slimy, chimney climbing is not majestic and the claustrophobia can be troubling. One friend tells me that stepping into these wedges within the crag feels like entering a tomb; light is restricted, the air is musty and sounds deadened. Another friend hates chimneys because he finds the movement desperately awkward and ungainly. Inside the crag, his hands and feet struggle to find holds while the metalware at his waist catches on the slightest nooks and edges. Eventually he emerges bruised, scraped, mucky and annoyed. A third friend absolutely loves chimneys and will dive into these tight spaces whenever the opportunity arises, relishing the thrutchy struggle that makes his partner curse.

Chimneying has an important place in climbing history. After the first climbers had explored the easy way up mountain crags, attention shifted onto a new aspect of steep rocky ground. From the 1880s, climbers began hunting out gullies and chimneys.[10] These early climbers had nothing like the range of sophisticated protection equipment that we have today. Hemp ropes were tied around waists and iron pitons were hammered into the wall. With limited equipment, gullies and chimneys were relatively safe. Slip or miss a move in a chimney and you shouldn't fall too far (although you might get wedged in an unpleasant position). A similar mistake on an open rock face could be fatal. For the pioneers, restriction enabled movement.

Inside chimneys, the rock presses in and you can press back – leaning, wedging, twisting and taking rests; the technical challenge is both interesting and awkward. Of course, trends change. Modern climbers often find chimneys baffling. 'Easy' chimneys can provoke streams of obscenities as adept gymnasts struggle to piece together the necessary moves to manoeuvre up 'hold-less' walls. Indoor walls provide little chance to practise three-dimensional full-body climbing.

Some gritstone chimneys hold unpleasant surprises. Imagine climbing inside a steep, green cleft of rock. Your hands and legs are stretched between two cool, damp walls; you push and shimmy upwards in a series of awkward and strangely strenuous moves. You huff and puff. Reaching up through the murky, fusty air for a ledge – finally, a good positive edge – your hand slides in something soft and squishy. A sharp, putrid stench rises. You withdraw your hand and wipe it on your trousers. Stinking white, green and brown gunk smears across your leg.

CLAP! CLAP!

Rock doves erupt from the ledge – wings beat loud – your heart leaps and pounds. You curse, tell your partner the route is 'fucking horrible', he reminds you that you chose it and tells you to get on with it. The ledge is yours now. You step up. The shelf is covered in downy feathers and heaps of shit. You curse again, hold your breath and reach up frantically, burning to take flight.

—

A trip into the bowels of a crag is not always unpleasant. One exceptionally hot summer day at Brimham Rocks, I was delighted to disappear up a cool, dark chimney. The air was thick as syrup and the fantastical rock formations were lapping up the heat. Will and I traipsed in over the heather moorland, weaving through the natural sculpture park, past leaning towers and perched boulders, flying saucers and hollow tubes, lava-lamp lumps and faces in the rock. We skirted around the Devil's Anvil, Castle Rock and Eagle Rock, neither of us in the mood to stop and squirm through Smartie Tube. We were bound for Lover's Leap, where two star-crossed Yorkshire lovers are said to have once jumped from the towering buttress. Edwin and Julia took this rash step when her father forbade their marriage and yet when they leaped, instead of plummeting to their doom, they floated gently down to the ground. Some say Julia's billowing skirts saved their fall; others put it down to fairies or some kind of magic within the rock itself.

At Lover's Leap, Will and I were both struggling, but our affliction was not one of romance. Recently back from Glastonbury, we were still feeling the effects of that heady spell of drink, dance and music. The rock, which had been so accommodating to Edwin and Julia, was less forthcoming with us. Sun lotion poured from my forehead into my eyes and, on the slabs, sweaty palms flapped about on sweaty stone. Craving relief, I headed up Lover's Leap Chimney.

From glaring sunshine to blinding darkness: my eyes took a few moments to adjust to the gloom. I had left behind the ferns and foxgloves at the foot of the cleft and moved up a polished crack, shimmying across into the vast hearth below the chimney proper. Inside, the ground was grubby. Grit, dust, twigs, plastic bottles and broken glass were strewn about the cavern, which was seldom swept clean. Dark passageways loomed, leading deeper into the crag. A caver might pursue these lines, pushing on into the blackness, intent on discovering the backstage architecture. But my way lay overhead. Far above there was a distant window. A skylight exit route. Like a young jackdaw hatched deep inside a chimney breast, I had to make my way up the flue to reach the light.

I slid in deeper. The rock closed around me. The sides of the chimney were polished smooth and, like the marble slabs inside an old dairy, deliciously cold. Hot hands reached and pushed against the walls, my sweaty back pressed on one side, my skin relishing every inch of contact with such cool rock.

Back and foot, I pushed up through the darkness. The trick was not to climb, but to push and wedge – levering between the opposing sides. With my back against one wall, I worked my feet up the opposite side. At first, I worried, but as I pushed on, gradually, the movement began to make sense. My vertical jostle found a rhythm. Muscles relaxed.

Higher up, the chimney widened and I stood – shifting weight from my back and onto my toes once again. Balance restored. The space brightened, light increased and when my hands reached up one last time they met the sun-warmed slopers. My upper body emerged, blinking and squinting. Heat radiated from the baking boulders. The bald summit dome was a furnace. I peeled off my tight rubber shoes and hurled them away. They landed in a nearby bush.

Gritstone climbing can be desperately trying, but between those intense passages up the rock face there are beautiful moments. Brontë country is not all bleak expanses and dour stones. Crawling off the rock at Hetchell, my hands and knees sank into a heavenly carpet of moss, roots and dirt and while Will climbed, I sat at the top, legs dangling over the edge, looking out over the treetops, enjoying rare views over the canopy. When the oaks came into flower, I watched flying insects hum between the pollen-laden tassels. Once, a peesie flew over, flapping heavily with its unwieldy black and white wings, uttering its gorgeous, gurgling, squeaking cry. *Pee-wit pee-wit pee-wit.* Flowers became wondrous. After the intense strain of trying to fathom a rock face, my mind could not quite comprehend such soft, delicate and colourful life forms as primroses, celandines and violets. How can such beings possibly exist in a world that can be as hard and brutal as rock?

With such moments, I sensed that something special happened when I spent time on rock. Climbing brought new perspectives. All of the fear, tension and focus altered my relationship to landscape. I was no longer the competent human – a detached observer – loping over the land with sure-footed confidence. On the rock, I could not pass over things with ease. During the moments of searing exposure, I pay incredibly close attention to the smallest of details. The nick inside a small crack. A fingernail flake of rock. Pimples and pebbles. Intense vulnerability sharpens the senses. But in the heat of the moment, it was difficult to hold on to these insights. As an apprentice, there was little space for nature appreciation: my time, focus and energy tended to be occupied by the demands of the climbing. Yet with time, as I learned the craft, the lens widened.

—

One May evening, Will and I headed out from Leeds to meet my friend Carl at Almscliff. Like me, Carl was also doing a literature PhD and, while passionate about his topic (Romanticism and mountains), he also relished the freedom it brought to get stuck into other things. At seminars and crags alike, he invariably showed up with an antiquated Karrimor rucksack full of books and/or climbing gear, an insulated flagon of tea and heaps of anecdotes. He started climbing in his early twenties and had since – together with his partner Rachel – been up the highest peak in every country in Europe, climbed in Yosemite and was in the process of becoming a prolific guidebook author. Born and raised in Bradford, he was also well versed in the local grit-stone crags and recited route names as though they were classic film titles. His tales of distinctive characters, unusual incidents and spectacular epics brought the rock to life.

In all my time indoors, I had barely touched on climbing culture or history. I didn't know the celebrities, famous crags or routes. I knew nothing of ethos or ethics. I was a gymnast who loved the movement and sociability of the sport and was now trying to take those elements out onto the rock. But outdoor climbing was profoundly different. There was a whole new vocabulary to learn, different techniques came into play and you had to become comfortable using a raft of equipment. Reading guidebooks, finding routes and following them up the rock was another skill set. And then there was also the wider environment and its changeable conditions to get a handle on. Attending to all of these aspects was tricky – essentially it amounts to an entire culture that I was completely ignorant of. Carl, by contrast, was steeped in this culture, and it showed.

Indoors, perhaps because there are so few other elements at play, huge emphasis can be placed upon the technical grade of a route, and many climbers are motivated by the desire to climb harder routes. Not Carl. He never climbs indoors. His self-professed motivation on the rock is, generally, 'to achieve very little'. With Carl, I gained a sense that climbing was an activity to be loved and embraced for all of its ridiculous, contradictory and frustrating quirks. Climbing did not have to be pursued as yet another puritanical route towards self-improvement or salvation. Rock was a medium for joy, play and struggle. You might 'fail' at a route, but you would gain a story. Whatever the outcome, by spending time on rock you were participating in a rich and wonderful culture that had evolved on some of the most challenging terrain in the UK. That night at Almscliff was a case in point.

Squeezing the car into a tight space on the hedge bank, we trampled up the field, anticipation mounting as we followed the drystone wall up to the rocky summit. Almscliff has an aura. The rocky fortress commands the low ridgeline above the Wharfe valley and is visible for miles. According to folklore, Almscliff was created during a fight between a giant and the devil. During the dispute, the devil picked up a stone and hurled it at Rombald of Ilkley Moor – but he missed, and the stone became Almscliff. In other versions of the tale the fight is not between Rombald and the devil, but Rombald and his wife; and it is she who hurls the creation stone. Such an origin myth connects Almscliff to the peaks of Ireland and Scotland, where the Cailleach legends tell of a giant woman who strode over the land wearing an apron filled with stones. When she dropped these rocks, they became mountains.

Sculpted by ice and water, the rocks of Almscliff have eroded into a labyrinth of round edges, clefts and deep fissures. At the top of the outcrop, huge weathered bowls cup rainwater, forming miniature pools that reflect the sky. The largest – Wart Well – was once used for healing. Early in the 1800s, you might have found J.M.W. Turner sat up here, sketching, when he was staying with his patron, Walter Fawkes at Farnley Hall. The Fawkes family (relatives of the notorious Guy Fawkes) had left their own impression on the rock. Across the most pronounced black fissure in the crag, pairs of opposing letters repeatedly appear, neatly engraved into the stone: TF | EL. TF was Thomas Fawkes of Farnley; EL was Edwin Lascelles of Harewood. The rift between the neighbours was not merely geological. During the era of transatlantic slave trade and West Indian plantations, the two estates occupied radically different ground. Walter Fawkes was a Whig and abolitionist who worked with William Wilberforce to pass the Slave Trade Abolition Bill in 1807; the Lascelles had made their fortune through the slave trade and numerous sugar plantations in Barbados and Jamaica.[11] An ambitious businessman, Henry Lascelles (1690–1753) was one of the first to run a sugar plantation in Barbados using African slave labour. His experiment worked – the model proved extremely lucrative and soon expanded to islands across the Caribbean, forming the basis for an international industry of immense wealth and immense suffering. When slavery was finally abolished in 1833, Henry Lascelles, 2nd Earl of Harewood, was not left out of pocket. He made successful compensation claims for his six plantations, worked by 1,277 slaves, receiving a payment of £26,307 (worth, in today's money, several million pounds).[12] And the legacy lives on. To this day, many Black people in Britain, America and across the Caribbean have the surname Lascelles or Harewood – names that circle back to letters stamped onto rocks in West Yorkshire.

Almscliff, sometimes referred to as God's Own Crag, also occupies a commanding position within climbing history. Many great climbers learned their craft on these steep gritstone walls, which became a popular climbing venue in the years before the First World War. Schoolboys, students and school teachers alike have been drawn to these rocks. Within this fortress, past legends – the Botterill brothers, Arthur Dolphin, Allan Austin and John Syrett – live on. Their legacies are set in stone and brought to life, time and time again, by the hopeful aspirants that venture up their lines. Great Western, Western Front and Wall of Horrors: the sculpted edges and cracked buttresses are emblazoned with many remarkable routes. That evening, the rocks hummed with desire, focus and frustration. Beneath a huge mellowing sky, climbers scuttled between problems, setting about boulders, chimneys, fluted columns and fearsome faces.

A couple of helmeted climbers in coloured trousers and T-shirts were tackling a great round glob of gritstone, under which lurked a small face with deep-set eyes and an open, toothless mouth. The Goblin.

'They don't bloody call it Arms-cliff for nowt!' panted the climber, who lay in a sprawled wedge on a ledge beneath a black overhang.

'You've done the hard bit,' the belayer called as the climber summoned the strength and courage to head up the final chimney. Below him, the goblin sneered and grimaced, awaiting the next contender.

Meanwhile, Will was wrestling with Zig-Zag Direct, arms thrust deep into the gaps between rounded blocks that weaved and twisted up towards the sky. The route was burly, three-dimensional and awkward, which seemed typical of Almscliff.

Inevitably, something went wrong.

I can't remember whether Will made the top or if he decided the route was too hard and backed off, but the problem shifted from climbing up the dark cracks and slabs to freeing a piece of gear. Our golden hex was wedged tight inside the crag. Almscliff would not give it up without a fight. Will pulled and tugged. The piece didn't budge. Will yanked harder, his face turning red. The hex still didn't move.

Fed up and flummoxed, Will cursed and Carl lowered him down, stepping forwards with overflowing enthusiasm: 'Belay me up! I'll give it a go.'

Where Will had grown bored, tired and frustrated, Carl stuck at it, trying all sorts of techniques to get the piece out. He climbed above and tugged; he bashed from below; he held on and jiggled. The position was tricky. The rock bulged in such a way that he could not hang on the rope and so his arms and calves were active all the time, holding him in position. Sometimes, removing gear can be far more strenuous than the climb itself.

'Pass us a pebble, I'll try hammering it out.'

I scouted around and threw a stone up to Carl. He began hammering. *Tap-tap tap-tap*. The hex didn't move. *Tap-tap tap-tap*. Dogged and determined, he stuck at it. *Tap-tap-tap-tap-tap-tap-tap.*

I grew tired just watching.

'Leave it, Carl.'

'I've almost got it!'

He hadn't.

'Honestly, it doesn't matter.'

'Maybe if I try this way.'

Eventually – at our insistence – Carl relented and agreed to be lowered without releasing the piece. Nonetheless, as we packed up for the night, he insisted that the piece was still salvageable. He was confident that another climber would zip up and miraculously lift the golden hex from the stone.

'I'll come up with Rachel and the kids next week. I bet you it'll be gone by then.'

Sure enough, by the following week, some mystery climber with even greater skill or tenacity had been and done the job. Excalibur had gone.

—

Looking back, my memories of Yorkshire climbing are full of mishap and emotion. As Will and I learned the craft of trad climbing, things often went wrong. We got stuck. We lost gear. Time disappeared with nothing to show for it. Gritstone climbing seemed to demand a thick skin and bloody-minded persistence. Struggling, flapping, falling and failing: I was often frustrated, disappointed or frightened on the rock. The simplest joy appeared away from the rock when the drama was all over and we went for a pint or an ice cream or bobbed around in the peat-browned River Wharfe.

Yet something kept drawing me back to the gritstone edges. The rock had an impenetrability that pulled me in, curious. It had a certain aura; a commanding character that

I wanted to open up. Working at those gritstone lines, pulling out moves and sequences to fit around the rock's folds, trying to access and understand its taciturn nature, I came to see how the gritstone brought my body to life in a way that nothing else did. Reaching into the cracks, curving my palms around the slopers, pushing, bridging and balancing, the textures of the tough gritty edges were writing themselves into my skin. Despite the scrapes and skirmishes, I craved the movement and contact. Eventually, at Henry Price I began to find some grace on the gritstone.

At the heart of Leeds University campus there is an old graveyard where grass, daisies, willows, sycamores and apple trees grow between a scattering of dark monuments and occasional gravestones. Just off-centre, a small Grecian temple of soft yellow sandstone is quietly turning green. This Victorian cemetery – a resting ground for some 97,000 people – was re-landscaped in 1969 to form a quiet, reflective garden space. With only a few entrance points in the stout, encircling gritstone walls, the garden is partially sealed off from the campus. While people are free to come and go, most students and many staff don't know this green space exists. It is the perfect haven.

On top of one section of the outer cemetery wall sits a 1960s student hall of residence. Designed by the architects responsible for other post-war classics such as the Barbican, this monolith of brick, concrete and glass is known as the Henry Price Residences (named after a Leeds businessman and philanthropist). Beneath this building, which offers shelter and lighting, the old cemetery wall has been developed into a climbers' crag. The challenge is to traverse from left to right, keeping to the black and grey gritstone blocks.

Pockets appear in the crumbling mortar between the blocks, forming the edges to which climbers' fingers and toes must cling. Some pockets are spacey; some are minute.

The Henry Price Wall (as it is known by climbers) was first developed in the 1970s and 1980s when buildering or brick-edge cruising became popular. Back then, before indoor climbing gyms became widespread, students from Leeds and Sheffield prowled their cities hunting for training opportunities that would help them build strength and technique for their weekend trips to the crags. Shopping centres, pubs and university walls all came into play. Wherever gaps consistently appeared in masonry, an in-situ climber might be found, building finger-strength on tiny crimps. While many of the old routes have since fallen out of use (and some have vanished through redevelopment), the tradition of Henry Price remains. The overhanging student flats make it an accessible 'all-weather' crag. Whereas shoppers in Headingley could be rather vocal in their disapproval of climbers there, for forty years lackadaisical students have mooched uninterestedly past the Henry Price climbers, allowing us to grunt over the blocks in peace.

When I first ventured onto these gritstone panels, I couldn't stay on for long. The tiny edges demand an intense fingertip grip. My arm muscles soon burned up and set hard as concrete. But with time and practise, my strength and stamina built. The problem, though, was not merely one of muscle. As with the best rock challenges, technique, rhythm and sequence were essential. Working and reworking the panels, falling off and stepping back on again, I stuck at the puzzle, returning again and again, determined to piece together the elaborate jigsaw.

In time, my feet learned to dance between the stones, taking advantage of the big spaces and moving swiftly over the tiniest edges. I knew where the rests were – places where the mortar had been chipped out from behind the blocks – providing deliciously deep handholds. Here, I might pause and hang, shaking my limbs, loosening lactic acid. With practise, I linked the moves, developing a glorious flowing traverse. Then, my hips hugged and swayed as I leaned into and out of the edges; fingers grasped and reached around the blocks; feet stepped and crossed, pointing and spanning. The piece was exact, demanding and beautiful.

—

Four years after the thunderstorm on Ilkley Moor, I came back to the Cow and Calf on another searing hot day. It was strange to be back. I had since moved away and developed my craft on other rocks and crags across the UK. But the gritstone had stayed with me. Those hard round edges and dark corners which I had so feared and loathed had somehow become fundamental. The rugged physical tussles had so shaped mind and muscle that it seemed as though one of those great round gritty blocks had settled somewhere deep within my being.

Wandering up into the quarry, I hungrily sought out the lines I had worked with Will and Carl. Walewska, Old Crack, Josephine. Everything was still there. Craning my neck to take in the green cracks and brown faces, the thrilling intensity of those gritstone evenings rushed back. My stomach flipped and churned, remembering bold leads and run-out edges.

Moving round to the Cow, I stood under her flank and breathed into that heaving mass of gritstone, letting the cliff tower over me. Fingers sought out the old nicks that they had clung to that evening of the thunderstorm. There. A line of chipped in-cuts running over the smooth face towards the great blocks far above. Reaching up, I placed my fingers in and brought my feet up off the ground. There. For a moment, I slotted back in and felt the surge of a memory reinhabited.

But this time, I would not be drawn up the cliff.

I left off the gritstone to follow my friend's footsteps as she wound up through the bracken and bilberries onto the open moor above. The rock faces that held my attention – which I scanned, searching out all the details; the bumps, slopes, nicks and cracks – did not speak to her in the same way. She was not a climber and we were not here to climb. We had no route planned. We might pad up the flagstones, following the pavement lifted from the old mills, now laid out end to end, tracing long dry lines across the boggy moorland. We might pass the Stanza Stones and head up to that curious stone circle, the Twelve Apostles. Then again, we might just drop back down, find a bench, have an ice cream and silently look out north. As one visits the beach, we had come to Ilkley Moor simply to be here.

Up on the moor, the grouse called out their strange guttural cries. *Getback-getback-getback.*

We scuttled around the top rocks, leaping across clefts, pausing to read some of the names and dates incised into the soft stone. Jas Marshall. J Bramley. EM Lancaster 1882. B E F 1940. Further on, we might hunt out older marks – cups, rings and swirling patterns appear on boulders strewn across the moor – simple etchings that have softened with time. Like the burial mound across the dale on Beamsley Beacon, these markings go back some 4,000 years, to the early farmers of the Neolithic-Bronze Age.

Insects hummed, grasshoppers ticked and a bumblebee trundled between flowers as we headed gently west. Drifting across the heather, harmonies came and went. Now rising; now fading. Was someone singing? I had never heard anything like it up here before. The chanted song seemed to rise from the earth itself, floating and drifting on the warm summer air. We wandered on, drawn in, mesmerised.

At the back quarry, we came to a stop. We had reached the source.

Below us a group was performing their own rocky ritual. This one involved no ropes, chalk or harnesses. Four women, one with a baby strapped to her back, stood in a line behind their male lead. Tucked away but highly conspicuous, in glaring contrast to the muted moorland palette, the group were dressed in brilliant white flowing gowns, with clean white caps covering their heads. I could not see their faces – for they were not offering their song out into the open quarry bowl, but rather, they faced in, singing upwards, towards a red rock face at the centre of which a shadowed enclave opened, leading further back into some hidden depth of the moor.

Call and response: the congregation echoed and repeated melodic phrases, creating rhythms and harmonies; their voices rising and falling together. They were Christian, probably, Ethiopian perhaps – this was a ceremony and a practice unlike anything I had come across before.

I wondered why they were addressing that particular piece

of rock. Did it represent something specific? An opening to something or somewhere else? Some form of high altar? The meaning was lost on me. I did not have the language or religion to make sense of this ceremony and yet I recognised the focus – that pouring of expression into the rock.

It was here that I began to grasp the depth of feeling that can move between people and rock. The gritstone edges of West Yorkshire had shown me how rock could knit bodies to the landscape. With touch, wit, imagination and ritual, the hard, gritty matter of those ancient riverbeds turned soft and malleable. Climbing, playing, singing, carving, quarrying, walking, storytelling – over millennia, person after person from generation after generation had made contact with these rocks, each bringing their own hopes, dreams, desires and histories to bear upon the stones, which likewise left their own impressions upon us. We mark the rock; the rock marks us.

Inside the quarried fold, sounds conjured from lung and tongue resonated and reverberated, glancing off the rock face, bouncing back out again to rise up, drifting into the open moorland air where the notes flowed and faded, an earnest human expression melding into heather and insect hum.

III

KALYMNOS

LIMESTONE

Continental crags can feel worlds apart from their British counterparts. At home, sometimes, the outdoor climbing world seems to be played out in various shades of grey. Grey rock, grey sky, grey hair, grey faces. Grey trees, grey rain, grey midges, grey sandwiches.

Meanwhile, in Spain, France, Greece and Italy, white and orange limestone routes line up under clear blue skies. Ditching waterproof, woolly hat and down jacket, you walk to the crag in shorts, vest and sandals. Your jumper stays in the bottom of your bag. Baguettes, bananas, salami, nuts and cheese replace pork pies and Tesco sandwiches. Forget tea and ale: this is the land of coffee and cold lager. *Attendez!* Goats clamber over boulders foraging for unattended snacks. All around, climbers of different ages and nationalities are engaged and stimulated: climbing, chatting, resting, smoking, watching.

My first taste of continental cragging took place on a Greek island. Just off the coast of Turkey, a mass of limestone rises from turquoise waters. On Kalymnos, cliffs and caves soar over beaches and white villas. Every morning, climbers leave their rented apartments on rented mopeds, travelling out across the island in pursuit of promising lines.

In summer, they seek the shaded north faces, and in winter they take to southerly aspects. Between times, every flank is occupied. When the sun slips back into the sea, the climbers descend from the crags. Glass clinks, routes are discussed and tales of triumphs and spectacular failures are retold in village bars below the darkening night sky. All along the streets, tables groan under the staggering weight of Greek hospitality, made material in platters of salad, olives, chips, bread, halloumi, stuffed peppers, grilled fish and moussaka.

Before Kalymnos became climbers' paradise, the rocks were seen as a curse. Islanders struggled to scratch a living off the steep, rocky slopes. Most of the island is barren. Instead, the Kalymniots made their living from the sea. For centuries, men plunged from boats into the warm Aegean waters to harvest sponges growing on the seabed which sold for good prices on the world market. Kalymniot divers were skilled experts and the island came to be known as the sponge-diving capital of Europe. However, in the 1980s, a marine virus decimated the sea sponge population. The island economy floundered. Emigration surged.

Then a visitor arrived who looked upon the island with a different eye. In 1996, an Italian climber on a summer holiday spotted the potential of Kalymnian rock. Returning the following year, Andrea di Bari began developing the first climbs, and things grew apace from there. Twenty years later, there are some 3,400 routes and counting (new routes are established at such a pace that guidebooks need frequent updates). Kalymniots embraced this reinvention of their island, providing apartments, bars, cafés, tavernas, gear and moped hire shops to meet the needs of climbing tourists.

With such welcoming hosts, good facilities and quality rock, Kalymnos is now a magnet for European climbers.

—

On the first morning of our week-long climbing holiday, the boatman took us from Kalymnos to the northern shore of Telendos, where we scrambled off the boat straight onto limestone. A short walk uphill brought us to the foot of our first crag, Irox. Ahead lay pale rock and slabs, black streaks and orange crevices, arêtes and edges. A child at Christmas, facing a mountain of unopened presents, I was wide-eyed and eager. From the white gravel and dirt at the base of the crag, I looked up to shining lines of bolts stretching up the rock to the final lower-off chains at the top. Like much climbing across mainland Europe, the routes on Kalymnos are 'sport' climbs, which means that bolts have been drilled into the rock to furnish each route with regular, secure protection. Bolts make climbing quicker and more efficient, with less time absorbed in the meticulous work of finding, placing and removing gear. But where to start? There were so many routes to choose from.

We began with routes where the intricate, easy-angled limestone offered plenty of holds. On Sally's Boat Trip, Captain Jack and Pantelis Sea Jump I bounded up the warm rock, fingers and feet finding ample purchase on the rough surface. Upon reaching a bolt, I took a quickdraw from my harness and clipped it on with the satisfying clink of metal on metal. Then I attached the rope and moved on. The limestone was different from the stuff I had climbed on in the UK. The lines were longer; the rock cleaner. Less loose.

There was a pleasing solidity that encouraged confidence, and sequences of pockets inviting me up the wall. But the stone was sharp. Razor edges pressed on my soft fingerpads, numbing sensation, grazing my palms and wrists, threatening to break the skin. I was careful not to pinch too tight and anxious not to slip. Sevasti, Evoula, Evangelina: each climb left its mark; in the evening I massaged beeswax balm into my sore fingertips.

At first we climbed as a herd – a great group of twenty friends, split into ten pairs that worked the rock with their own rope and set of quickdraws.

We shouted advice and encouragement to one another, giving tips on routes, laughing and revelling in the sunshine.

'Nice moves, Beth!'

'Try this one next – it's awesome!'

As the day progressed and we found our feet, the herd spread. My partner and I moseyed along the rock faces, sampling routes like the opportunist island goats that paused to snaffle our tasty treats. After Lucas Bad Boy, Hot Roc and A l'Ovest di Kaboul, we rounded a corner where another crag emerged, unlike anything I had ever seen before.

Here the climbers pulled themselves up orange pillars, columns and stalactites on angles that were rarely less than vertical, and much was overhanging. We watched in awe. These were serious climbers, tackling extreme routes on extraordinary features. This was tufa climbing. Before my week on Kalymnos, I had never heard of tufa. By the end, I was obsessed.

Picture a wine bottle on a table in a French restaurant. The wine has long since been drunk and the bottle now serves as a candle holder, with the glass all but disappeared beneath streams of dripping wax which cluster in cascades, runnels and globules. Layers of wax reveal the passage of time, as candle after candle melts and sets into new shapes on the remains of those that came before. The form is grotesque and fascinating. This is tufa in miniature. Tufa (pronounced too-fah) forms when water, saturated with limestone minerals, runs over a surface and the chemicals precipitate out of the liquid. Over time, the chemical deposits build up into substantial layers – producing new mounds, pillars, cushions, columns and other intricate shapes.

The immense tufa formations on Kalymnos transform the cliffs into gothic cathedrals. On the steepest rocky edges, you look up to spires, pointed arches, vaults, buttresses and ornate decoration. The architecture celebrates ascent: each intriguing protrusion leads upwards into another in a soaring schema of verticality. Yet the scale and angles are fearsome. In the Grande Grotte, your neck aches and your mind spins as you peer up to watch climbers moving far overhead, hanging spider-like from stalactites, clipping the rope through bolts drilled into the immense arched roof.

Such routes are far beyond my ability – but I can still marvel at the experts. Tanned muscles ripple and flex as Czech, Greek, French, Spanish, Italian, Polish, Korean, Japanese and American climbers work their way up the impossible. Some climb topless, others stripped down to sports bra or bikini. Backs shine with the strain, mouths grunt and shout, but the climbers remain focused and flexible. Legs stretch into immense bridges, toes press on gnarled tufa, hands reach and grasp. Inside, a fire burns. Again and again the climbers summon the strength to push on, energy blazing from their beating core as they move from one impossibility to another. These are the rock gods.

Climbing up into the grotesque architecture, I explored the tufa for myself. The dripping rock forms protruded from the facade like saints and gargoyles carved into ancient churches and cathedrals. But their features were all distorted. Twisted. Melted. Jumbled. The curve of an ear appeared beside a gaping mouth. There was a hollow cheek. Some teeth. A long tongue. Empty eye sockets. Feathered wings.

The saints were encouraging. They reached out from the wall, offering good holds, such as deep pockets, sequences of nodules or huge round handles, lovingly referred to as 'jugs'. These blessed features provided rest stances and enclaves into which I could wedge a knee and lessen the strain for a moment. But hidden among the saints were gargoyles. These slippery features mocked and repelled climbers. The perfect pocket could be tantalisingly close, yet infuriatingly out of reach. Or the promising cascade turned out to have no proper holds, just rounded edges that my sweaty, overworked hands struggled to grasp.

A few days into the trip, I watched one of our group have a particularly memorable run-in with the tufa saints and gargoyles. A strong climber, he was keen to push his grade on a route called Cyclops. Our Odysseus eyed the route warily, knowing that this would be a fearsome opponent. This twenty-metre line runs up the edge of an orange cave brimming with gnarled protrusions before moving up onto a grey wall with a few pockets. The climb finishes high above at a huge black hole: the eye of the Cyclops.

I stepped forward. 'Shall I belay?'

'Best not,' he replied, fastening his shoes and warily eyeing the way ahead. 'If I fall, you'll fly.'

A bigger guy stepped up to take the rope, lacing a pair of hefty leather walking boots in preparation. I settled into the shade beneath the steep walls to watch the drama unfold.

That week, these men had become my climbing crew. The four of us (three men, one woman) formed a tight group, talking each other through routes, belaying and shouting encouragement. Observation was everything: we learned from the constant flow of success and failure. There were routes that all four of us struggled at, climbing on a tight top rope, trying again and again to get up. Again and again, we fell off and hung on the rope, gasping for breath, shaking pumped limbs and studying the hot rock before swinging in to try again. We watched one another's attempts closely. Each climber brought something different. With the use of an undercling, a heel hook or a distinct angling of the hips, they might unlock an entire new sequence.

On Cyclops, the climber led boldly up the wall, grasping tufa formations, moving with strength, dexterity and power. He weaved over the cave roof following rocky florets. The climbing was strenuous. He sweated, cursed and shook out his arms. We were with him, watching every move, willing him on.

'Come on!'

'Nail it!'

Over the cave, the tufa shrank. The number of holds thinned, demanding bigger moves across blank walls. Hands dived into the chalk bag tied to his waist, pummelling the powder for grip. Acid burned in his pumped forearms. Adrenaline surged. He became jittery.

'You've got—'

'Shut up!'

He needed a rest but – unable to find one on the steep ground – he pushed on with frantic determination to the next bolt.

The bolt came into reach. A shaking hand grabbed for a quickdraw and stretched up to the shining ring in the rock. There was the clink of metal: he had attached the quickdraw. The hand reached down for the rope, drawing a great loop up to the clip. Relief was in sight. But then – he dropped the rope. And his arms failed.

Like a dead weight, he plunged for four or five metres. Then the rope caught in the bolt below, the belayer was wrenched off his feet and both men were hurled into the rock face. The climber returned to earth and we clustered in. A new graze glistened on his elbow and a vivid red streak trickled down his shin from a scab that had been torn from his knee. Cyclops had chewed him up and spat him out.

We slapped his sweaty back and shouted praise, because this fall was no tragedy. This was not a crushing defeat. He might have failed at the route, but he had taken a huge risk and climbed right out of his comfort zone. Sometimes, failure is better than success.

Risk is integral to being human. Stepping out of the front door, talking to strangers or family members, applying for a new job, starting or ending a relationship: all of these acts can be risky. Of course, what feels dangerous to one person is within the comfort zone of another. Risk is intensely personal and subjective. As children develop and learn about their place in the world, they play with risk. They climb trees, get into mischief and test boundaries. With these acts, the outcome is unknown: they might make it up the tree; they might not. They might get into trouble; they might not. Circumstances may be improved; they may not. Risk takes you into the sphere of uncertainty, which can be a difficult space to inhabit. But fear of risk is paralysing. I have seen many people get stuck in difficult places (both on and off the rock) because they are afraid to take a chance.

Climbing provides a good space to continue exploring risk as an adult. On the wall, you repeatedly climb into uncertainty. Sometimes you pull off new moves and routes with ease, sometimes you don't. Failing can be difficult. The emotions of failure are hard to stomach. But the best climbs are those where the outcome is uncertain. And so you must learn to handle the disappointment, frustration and embarrassment of failure. A good climber does not eliminate risk: they harness its electrifying charge.

—

All that week, we played with risk, repeatedly pushing ourselves and climbing into uncertainty because in the sunshine, in brilliant and inspiring company, failure did not taste bitter. Failing was part of the fun. As well as grunts, shouts and cursing, the air around the crags rang with laughter, chatter and song. And the risks took place on and off the rock. The mopeds that we hired to zip around the island could be just as treacherous as climbing. Take a corner too fast and the gravel had the bike out from underneath you. Take another bend at the right speed and you might still have to brake suddenly when you happened upon a herd of indolent goats lounging on the road. Should it all get to be too much, if we did grow hot, tired and flustered and couldn't bear to look at the blazing rock face any longer, we did not have to go far to cool off. Then we rolled down to the sea and basked in the warm waters at Arginonta, letting our hot muscles unravel while a new thirst grew upon us that was soon quenched at the nearest bar with a bottle of cold Mythos as the sun set.

Even at the bars, as the woozy haze of sunshine and alcohol set in, climbing stayed at the forefront of our minds and conversation. We were beached in a heavenly dreamscape of hot, beautiful limestone. At the end of a good day, we watched the sun leave the rocks, knowing it would return again tomorrow. Alongside that contented daze, ambition flickered and flared. Watching the experts at work on the Mediterranean limestone, a new world had opened and I desperately wanted to climb harder, taking on new challenges and leading big routes up steep faces.

'You should try Perskindol,' recommended Luke on one such evening, as we looked out across the sea from the Pirate Bar. Luke was the strongest climber of our quartet who, with over twenty years' experience, climbed like a skilled workman. He had been to Kalymnos before and proved an excellent guide that week, consistently leading us – his eager apprentices – onto interesting and demanding lines at crags across the island. His recommendations carried great weight and so, just like that, tomorrow's goal was set.

The next morning, Luke led us up to the limestone escarpment that towers over Masouri. Panting up the steep slopes, we left the village behind, following a thin path weaving through rock, grit, thyme, gorse and grey, thorny bushes. Battered goat fences bisected the rough scrub. Hard to imagine how these thin, rusted wires could hold the wily creatures in; nonetheless, we closed the gates behind us. Passing a single olive tree with a gnarled, cracked grey trunk, I was suddenly reminded of hawthorns on the sheep-grazed hills of home. Like stubborn old grandmothers, these gnarled trees speak of long lives borne in harsh circumstances, sustained by a shrewd resourcefulness and the ability to take advantage of the thinnest soils.

'Not far now,' Luke called, cheerily.

At the immense rock face of Ivory Tower, we skirted the base of the cliff. The crag was quiet. Perhaps we were early. Unlike the overhanging walls elsewhere on the island, this cliff was not dripping with tufa pillars and columns. Instead, the limestone was rough and intricate, soaring up in huge sweeps of grey, black and orange. Where the escarpment folded into the hill, the smell of goat grew stronger. Inside the pungent enclave, at chest height we found red and black letters daubed onto the rock face. PERSKINDOL 6b+. We dumped our rucksacks, gulped water and flaked the rope.

This was my test piece. My Cyclops. But there could be no slips, no falls, no sitting on the rope: I was determined to lead-climb Perskindol clean.

Before launching into the unknown, I looked up, assessing the rock, arming myself with as much prior knowledge as possible. The route was long, steep and urgent. There were three sections: a lower pillar of pocked grey rock, a broken, overhanging roof of fiery orange and the upper grey walls that stretched on into the thorn bushes far overhead. I couldn't make out the chains at the top.

To successfully pull off such a big, demanding route

requires a certain headspace. A climbing body is not just muscle and limb: mind and emotion are also important. Watching Luke prepare to lead challenging routes, I noticed the journey he went through as he sought to enter the right headspace. Even with his level of skill and experience, the demanding climbs still triggered many intense and contradictory emotions. Hope, fear, desire, ambition and doubt swirled about. The right frame of mind is essential to cope with the unavoidable stress of pushing your limits.

'Smash it!'

'Nail it!'

'Fucking go for it!'

Our battle cries bounced around the slabs and tufa. This was the language that we three apprentices turned to at moments of stress. Like Popeye's tins of spinach, we used these outpourings to spur the climber on, helping them to summon the energy to keep going and smash the rock. Fear and doubt must be beaten into submission.

But Luke did not endorse this macho language. He had a sense that a different headspace could be used to approach hard rock challenges – a space that was quieter, less combative, more Zen. We apprentices were open to the idea, but a little perturbed. We knew how to test out different physical techniques – a simple matter of watching and copying other people's movements – but how do you adopt a different state of mind?

We conceptualised this Zen state by contrasting two famous climbers: Adam Ondra and Chris Sharma. Ondra is an expressive climber who screams, grunts and shouts under pressure. Sharma is the archetypal stoner dude who describes climbs in gentle mellifluent tones. Ondra became our battle-cry mindset; Sharma was our Zen master. At Luke's prompting, I tried to be Sharma: cool, collected and at one with the rock.

'Love the rock, don't smash the rock,' became our mantra, playfully voiced in American stoner drawl.

Wiping the dust from my shoes, I clambered onto the first black deposition streaks. The rock rose sharp, but there were plenty of positive features scattered across the coloured stone. Fingers found pockets and small jugs; toes pushed off edges. The dance began. Time to manipulate physics and hold off gravity. My body sprang into action, bridging between distant points of connection. Muscle and mind found its method; rhythm settled in.

'Go on, Anna!'

As I moved, sounds pressed in. From the village far below came the whine of mopeds. Hammering. A cockerel. Occasional bursts of dogs barking. When the heightened sensory state kicks in on the rock, sounds can become painfully intense. Earlier in the week, at the crux of another challenge, my head filled with surging seawater. The waves, which had been breaking unnoticed on the rocks below us for most of the morning, suddenly seemed to be crashing right inside my skull, as though my head had been hollowed out and transformed into a spiral seashell, echoing and amplifying sound.

Such moments displace habitual ways of inhabiting the world. In 'normal' life, I tend to occupy places filled with sounds that I can comfortably ignore. Traffic, chatter, birdsong, keyboard tapping, sheep cries or snatches of other people's music: when sounds carry information that I do not need to know, they become noises that I filter out. But during the intense fear and focus of climbing, that customary cultural practice of selective hearing is strained. The animal within stirs. In a moment, thousands of years vanish and I hear with the acute sensitivity of my ancestors. With instincts tuned in, braced to detect urgent notes, a curtain is lifted. I glimpse how other creatures might experience the world. Hare, wolf, bird or whale: unlike many modern humans, these creatures cannot afford to switch off from the sound-scape. Predator or prey: animals listen to survive. When climbing removes the cotton wool from my ears, sounds hit me with the intensity of lightning.

At the top of the grey pillar, I came face to face with the blazing orange overhang. Arching my spine and leaning out from the wall, I tried to take in as much as possible. The way ahead was steep and committing. Once I went for it, I would need to keep going, pulling up through the broken roof in a sequence of powerful moves. There could be no delay, no getting in a flap. If I kept steady, I would reach an island of easier ground some five metres hence.

Love the rock, don't smash the rock.

Shaking my arms out, I dipped my fingers into the chalk, exhaled and committed. Arms pulled into underclings and reached for bulging nodules, feet stretched and pushed, heels hooked and released, hips twisted and flexed. There were plenty of features sunk into the burnt-marmalade rock, the task was to link and continue. Keep going! With a high right foot and rock-over, I pulled up, heaving and gasping into a vertical wall. I had done it!

From here, the route continued weaving up through peach-grey rock, on and on up the face, meandering towards the distant chains. My heart pounded. Lungs, forearms and calves were at boiling point but there was still so much more required of me. This was a long route. I could feel the panic rising, drawing me into an exhausted, anguished fight. If I were to pull it off, I needed to hold the panic down, keep focused and summon yet more poise and strength. I desperately wanted a breather – some time out – a chance to gather myself. Temptation rose. It would be so easy to let go of the rock now and escape its relentless demand by resting on the rope. But then I would have to swallow the bitter taste of disappointment. I wanted to climb the route as I had intended. Clean.

From far below, a voice called up, 'Can you get to that block?'

I turned: to my right, at the edge of the rock face, a dark corner fell back into a black cleft. Within the cleft, a huge limestone block was jammed tight. Instead of resting on the rope, I could perch there. Swerving slightly off route, I made a beeline for the cleft. The work paid off. Sinking into the grimy darkness, I was soothed by the cool support and solidity of the block. I had found the perfect haven.

Time passed, my body recovered and the relief began to wane. I lingered on the grubby limestone lump, prolonging the rest, reluctant to move on, convincing myself that I was still climbing. Technically, after all, I was still 'on rock'. But really this was shadow play. Crawling into the dark refuge to escape the demands of the wall, I had imprisoned myself in Plato's Cave. Now I dreaded the return to the rock face and all of its glaring uncertainties. But the challenge that I had set my heart on lay outside the cleft. Summoning courage and steely willpower, I left the cave.

'Nice one Anna, you've got this!'

The first moves were desperately unpleasant. Why was I

here? Hands fumbled for holds, legs filled with doubt. Could I go back? I continued slowly, and slowly mind and muscles softened once again, shaping up to meet the task at hand. Rhythm returned. Mind sank into stone.

On the upper wall, the bolts were much further apart. Between clips, the spaces of uncertainty expanded. But, reconciled to my ambition, I hunted out features, keeping calm. Steady. The end was in sight. Come on. Smash it to the top.

Finally, with a rattle, I reached the chains, secured myself and squealed with delight. Below, the boys yelled and whooped. The dance was done.

—

What happened on Perskindol? Did I pull off the Zen mindset? No. The style appealed but the method was beyond me. It was years before I learned to hush the flailing ego and still the inner voices. For years after my trip to Kalymnos, when hard rock loomed and holds escaped my grasp, when the fear of falling mingled with the fear of failure, I could not be Zen. Then the rock was a terrifying adversary. My temperature soared and things became brutally black and white: fight or flight; defeat or be defeated. While I did not pull it off first time, our playful characterisation gave me an invaluable glimpse of another way to be on the rock. With time and a very particular personal experience, eventually, I found a way to become more calm, composed and meditative on the rock. At that point, my climbing changed. When the rock ceased to be a dangerous antagonist, climbing was no longer a battle; it was an encounter.

Leading Perskindol clean could be read as a moment of triumphant self-realisation. Fear and doubt were cast aside: I found the strength, courage and skill to master a rock climb at my limit. That sort of narrative tastes good: we love to consume stories of heroic endeavour; of an individual digging deep, discovering inner strength and realising personal potential. But something quite different happened on Perskindol. Perskindol was not self-realisation: it was a performance. On Perskindol, I successfully performed the collective climbing body.

At those busy limestone crags I was a sponge, soaking up technique, style, personality and language from everyone around. From my quartet, I learned about physical technique and head game. We studied one another in action, examining how the climber pulled off move after move on desperate ground. (Focus on footwork; take advantage of rests; use your legs.) Jumping on the rope and clambering up the wall, we mimicked one another, emulating each other's bodies to reach for success. Since we were constantly in the company of many different climbers – of all ages, sizes, nationalities, strengths and abilities – strangers also became a precious source of inspiration. Working our way around different crags over the week – Panorama, Ghost Kitchen, Secret Garden, Pescatore – I began to recognise faces. Again and again, a particular pair of French climbers appeared. In their early twenties, the two women worked hard routes up steep orange tufa faces. Their style was distinctive and impressive. We never spoke, but watching them climb was a game changer.

At that time I was climbing a lot in bouldering gyms with a crew of male friends. Like the sport climbing in Kalymnos, we had fun showing one another moves. There was also, always, a competitive edge to our climbing. The competition was exciting; it drove us to climb harder, pushing ourselves to try more difficult problems and develop greater technical skill. But I was often frustrated. In the hyper-performative space of indoor bouldering gyms, I hated failing. Especially on routes that my friends blazed up.

At those moments, when I had to cope with the difficult feelings of failure, my brain, hardwired to look for patterns, leaped to the most obvious and simple connection. I couldn't do the route. My male companions could. Then, in that state of miserable dejection and frustration on the bouldering mats, I felt my gender most painfully.

Feeling incompetent, I watched their male bodies move on the wall and compared myself to them, unfavourably. I saw their height and arm span and told myself that climbing was easier for men since they generally have a longer reach. I studied their muscle mass – their honed arms, broad shoulders, strong backs and powerful legs – admiring that brawny masculine strength that could never be mine. I looked at their hands and saw bigger palms and fingers that could hold tighter for longer. When things got difficult and my male companions pulled through steep ground using a rush of power that I did not seem to possess, I attributed it to testosterone. This gendered perspective took the colour from my climbing. I had imported a set of cruel binaries and constructed a tight-fitting corset for myself, telling myself that I couldn't climb as well as my male friends because I was a girl.

But on Kalymnos I realised gender was not a handicap. The French women were not troubled by their female bodies:

they blazed up routes far beyond the ability of any of my male climbing partners. On the ground, they stood a little shorter and stockier than me. On the rock, they moved fluently, using imaginative sequences to reach holds that lay beyond them. They had distinctive style and exceptional technique. Watching these women pull off move after move, I realised that I had it all wrong. The female body is not a barrier to top-class climbing. Our bodies can move with amazing strength and fluidity.

Now, when pushing my climbing grade, I look to girls and women as well as men. I love watching women climb, delighting partly in the sheer novelty of it – I still see too few women out lead climbing at the crags – but there is more to it than this. I love seeing a woman tackle tough physical challenges, sticking with problems and harnessing her individual strengths to pull off difficult sequences. Seeing a woman climb, I discover the power of the female form. Women teach me to climb differently. Our bodies are different and so we benefit from particular techniques. Small fingers can be an advantage: as well as slotting our hands into narrow openings, our fingers often find new holds on seemingly blank faces. Tiny crimps and edges can become key details that uphold the female climbing body, enabling us to move up the wall in unique style. In climbing, strength to weight ratio is more important than muscle mass. We often have a lighter frame – making it easier for our fingers to carry our weight on those tiny edges. Flexibility is also on our side: we can bend, twist and curl fluidly around features. I love watching a skilled woman approach a challenging problem that has been occupying a number of grunting, thrusting men. She pauses, examines the features and then hops on, revealing a new intricate sequence of fluent movement, solving the problem with graceful ease.

Yet a female climber does not only have a different physical form; our bodies are also influenced by a distinct set of hormones. While we have some testosterone – the hormone of strength and power – our monthly cycle is more significant. For a long time, I felt that my cycle of changing moods, energy and concentration levels was a hindrance to my climbing. How could I develop as a climber when some weeks I was strong and optimistic and on other weeks I was bloated, tired, sweaty and angst-ridden? This rollercoaster seemed worlds apart from anything my male climbing partners went through. They all seemed to operate on a steady baseline. Comparing myself to men, once more I came up short.

The trouble with living in a man's world is that anything that deviates from the (male) norm is poorly understood and can be considered a deficiency. Historically, there has been a real lack of understanding around how women's bodies respond to sport and exercise. We have been kept out of research and clinical trials because we have too many physiological variables.[13] It is easier and cheaper to work with men and so advice on nutrition and training models are built around the male body. But all that is changing. The taboo is breaking and across the sporting world, research and practice are starting to take women seriously. With this new interest, we are beginning to see that the female hormonal cycle need not be a barrier to athletic performance.[14]

In casual chatter with other female climbers, I discovered that for some of us, our climbing was transformed when we came off the contraceptive pill. For years, I liked taking the pill. Those little tablets levelled out my monthly hormonal fluctuations, but when I stopped, I found I had been living in a constant fog. Off the pill, my energy levels improved significantly: I suddenly had much more stamina, confidence and a better capacity to think in stressful situations. While for some women the pill is the right choice, it was not right for me.

Another woman told me that the summer she came off the pill, she went from having led a handful of E1 routes to leading E4: a remarkable progression. For her, it is all about the head game: the pill made her feel like she had premenstrual syndrome (PMS) all the time. (This is the week before your period comes, when your body becomes tense and difficult emotions surge.) While PMS is different for every woman – some get no symptoms at all – generally speaking, this part of the cycle does not provide the best physical and psychological space to push yourself. Anticipating that week and learning to take it easy is a game changer. Just as the sea-cliff climber tracks the tide, keeping an eye on conditions to find the perfect window to get out onto certain routes, so the science now says that a sportswoman can perform better with a personal understanding of her cycle. Knowing when to be gentle and when to go for it can make all the difference.

As I began to appreciate the real strengths and abilities of women climbers, a novel idea dawned on me. Perhaps women can actually climb harder than men. I looked into the statistics in the world of graded sport climbing. Men are ahead, but women are catching up. Two men have climbed 9c (Adam Ondra and Chris Sharma) and a handful have climbed 9b+. Two women have now climbed 9b: nineteen-year-old Laura

Rogora in July 2020 and Angela Eiter in 2017 (eight months prior to this, Margo Hayes led the first female 9a+). Since climbing, historically, has been a male-dominated sport, the pool from which the top male athletes are drawn is much larger. But that is changing. Fast. As more and more women enter the sport, the gender gap is closing.

Chatting to a friend about all of this, I asked her whether she thinks women will ever climb harder than men. She laughed.

'We already have.'

In 1993, Lynn Hill became the first person to free climb the Nose of El Capitan in Yosemite. Alison Hargreaves was the first person to solo the six major Alpine north faces in a year. In 2008, Beth Rodden put up a new route called Meltdown in Yosemite. At the time, Meltdown was the hardest single-pitch trad climb in America. The route remained unrepeated for over ten years, despite some of the best climbers in the world trying it.

IV

CUILLIN I

GABBRO AND BASALT

Epic

1. *A long poem, typically one derived from ancient oral tradition, narrating the deeds and adventures of heroic or legendary figures of the past history of a nation*
2. *An exceptionally long and arduous task or activity*
3. *Heroic or grand in scale or character*

Ask a poet or a scholar about an epic and they might cite Homer, Virgil, Dante or Milton. Some might recite lines from *The Odyssey* or *Paradise Lost*. Others might talk about the hero narrative and oral storytelling cultures; explaining how long poems were used to record history and establish national identities. Ask a climber – the right climber – and their eyes will roll before they lean forwards, with a slight grin, to tell you their tale. Or tales, as the case tends to be.

An epic, in climbing, refers to a particular type of experience. It is distinct from 'epic' as adjective, wherein the word is uttered with gusto to express great enthusiasm for something, as in 'Siiick – that climb looks epic!' A climbing epic (noun) indicates a more complex experience: a climb that was long, hard and problematic for any number of reasons.

In a sport where you learn by doing – and doing means putting yourself into challenging situations – inevitably things go wrong. Mistakes happen. On any given rock climb, there are plenty of things to misjudge: weather, timing, the scale and technical challenge of the undertaking, how much to pack, your ability. When these misjudgements start to stack up, often compounded by a significant external factor, then you are heading into epic territory.

A climbing epic is not fun at the time, but for storytellers, it can become fun in retrospect, when reframed to form an entertaining narrative. There can be an element of bragging within epic-story culture, particularly in younger climbers who consider an epic to be a rite of passage. They will recite their story, loud and proud, wearing it as a badge of honour, signalling their initiation into the climbing fraternity.

The first climbers that I came into contact with were young men who delighted in recounting epic stories; but their ale-fuelled outpourings of heroic masculinity did not enrapture their entire audience. Listening to these rudimentary tales, I was not overly impressed. I had not been brought up to celebrate peril or hardship in the same way – to laugh off accidents, injuries and near-misses. I approached risk differently. I was more cautious, and this inherent cautiousness was endorsed by wider social messaging. When approaching the mountains, *be careful* was the message I was given, again and again. (I always wondered whether I would be given that same line, with such insistent regularity, if I was a man.) Thus the epic-story culture, which seemed to inspire certain young men to go forth braced with hearty doses of bravado, ready to boldly meet their own misadventures on the rocks, did not have the same effect on me. In fact, it was rather the opposite. If, as these stories suggested, the quintessential traditional climbing experience was a macho epic, then traditional climbing was not for me. How could I seriously pursue an activity for which I lacked the balls, so to speak?

With time though, I came to discover that an epic does not have to be a statement of heroic masculinity. Older climbers tend to deliver their stories more quietly – with twinkling eyes and sardonic finesse – acknowledging that they probably should have known better, but still, somehow, these things happen. A climbing epic can be troubling and profoundly humbling, and so the story can serve as debrief: a way of processing difficult incidents. Epics also function as cautionary tales. Of Carl's many epics, the story which begins with the line, 'It's wet anyway, let's go and do the Clachaig Gully!' has kept me, for the time being, safe, dry and well clear of that slimy hellhole. Epic stories thereby can become a vehicle, within the oral culture of climbing, for sharing problems, passing on information and learning from mistakes. After all, the best climbers are well versed in failure.

While certain people are more prone to epic experiences, so certain types of climbing lend themselves more to epic than others. It is hard to imagine the modern boulderer, sport or indoor climber having an epic. (Perhaps the whole concept is absent from their discourse?) By contrast, winter climbing is ideal. Depending on your ambition and skill level, traditional rock climbing sits somewhere in the middle, although certain places have an uncanny propensity for triggering epics. The Cuillin on Skye is one of those places.

—

On a fine evening in Applecross, stand on the beach and gaze out west. Across the sound you will see a chain of distinctive peaks rising from a dark island. The serrated black mountain – or mountains – scores a sharp line against the horizon. This is the Cuillin, a landmark across this region of bog, island, hill and sea at the northwestern fringe of Europe. The form is unmistakable, but the mood changes frequently. Sometimes, the peaks and points tumble in and out of a surging mass of grey-white cloud. Sometimes, the entire ridge vanishes in a thicket of dark storms. Soaring up from the Atlantic, this rocky mass consolidates the atmospheric stirrings of that great ocean.

The Cuillin, with its imposing form of many moods and aspects, has drawn in countless dreamers and visionaries, from visual artists to poets, musicians, photographers and writers. To climb in the Cuillin is to throw yourself into a rocky realm of epic resonance. The roll-call of eminent literary visitors includes Samuel Johnson, James Boswell, Sir Walter Scott and Lord Tennyson. In 1831, Turner journeyed up from the south and painted Loch Coruisk and the mountains in a swirling vortex of rock, water and cloud. The infamous mountaineer, occultist, magician, poet, painter and novelist Aleister Crowley first discovered rock climbing on a trip to Skye with his mother in 1891. Among the more local voices, Sorley MacLean, a poet who grew up on the neighbouring isle of Raasay, offers a radical vision of the ridge. His Gaelic epic, *An Cuilithionn*, draws on the forceful stature of his local hills to provide the grounds to lead the fight against fascism. Written in 1939 as a great darkness swept across Europe, MacLean dreamed the ridge into an awesome, shape-shifting symbol with the power to drive the international resistance to oppression in all forms.

> *A day and I in the rocky Cuillin,*
> *I heard the great pipe incited,*
> *roaring of mankind answering,*
> *brain and heart in harmony.*
>
> *I heard a cry on the mountains,*
> *the liberty-shout of the people rising.*[15]

———

When I first set foot on the ridge, I felt I had arrived on another planet. Cloud pressed in, obscuring the edges, chilling the body and removing reference points. There was no view, no perspective, no depth. Walls and boulders loomed through the mist, shimmering like apparitions, blurring like holograms. Loose stones slid, grating and grinding underfoot, but beyond the constant close-quartered crunch and rattle, sounds were deadened. No water flowing, no bird song. Everything was rough, sharp, grey and rocky.

Moving on through the gloom, small clearings emerged in the debris. Here and there the stones had been shifted aside, creating oblongs of red, gravelly earth the length of a human body. This series of savage resting grounds appeared like rough mountain sarcophagi, lining the way up to Sgùrr nan Eag.

Between the rhythm of my breath, heartbeat and each heavy footfall, a question grated, relentlessly droning through my psyche.

What the hell was I doing here?

—

I first came to the Cuillin in my early twenties, back when I was not much of a climber. At that point, my mountain craft was still in its early phase of patchy experience. My navigation was average: I could read a map and, when necessary, do compass bearings, but my preference was generally to leave the responsibility of route-finding to others. My rope-work was poor: I could tie in and belay but somehow, whenever I handled ropes in the outdoors, they ended up in the most terrible tangle. Time was lost and tempers frayed as we were forced to flake fifty or sixty metres of dynamic woven nylon again and again, running the ropes through to pull out the knots and let the line run smoothly. I had occasionally lead-climbed short gritstone routes at Stanage and Froggatt, but before setting foot on the Cuillin, I had never abseiled.

What I lacked in experience though, I made up for with enthusiasm. I loved charging up the hills with a crew of good friends. On ridgelines like Crib Goch on Snowdon and Càrn Mòr Dearg Arête on Ben Nevis, I had discovered the joys of un-roped scrambling. On those narrow rocky lines each hand and foot placement mattered, and I loved the commitment and focus demanded by such serious terrain. I relished the delicate play between nerve and physical technique. The atmosphere of such defined glaciated edges was startling, particularly in combination with the erratic British mountain weather system. Sometimes staggering views opened out to the valleys far below my feet, sometimes wind blasted across the edges, forcing me to hug the rock and hold on tight, sometimes the view was obscured by mist – then the ridges materialised and vanished, seen as a sequence of peaks and knolls coming in and out of the clouds like ghostly apparitions. With such an inclination for the thrilling mystique of a mountain ridgeline, it was only a matter of time before I should find myself on the Cuillin.

The Ridge, as the Cuillin is often termed by mountaineers, is a twelve-kilometre crest of rocky peaks that is held to be the ultimate British mountain ridge. In its entire length, the Ridge never drops below 2,500 feet (762 metres) and fourteen of the peaks rise to over 3,000 feet (914 metres). One of those peaks, named the Inaccessible Pinnacle or In Pinn for short, holds the prestigious acclaim of being the only Munro in Scotland that requires a rock climb to reach the summit. The scale of the challenge is beyond anything else found on our shores. Most walkers break the commanding line down into smaller, manageable sections, climbing up sharp from Glen Brittle, the Sligachan or Loch Coruisk to bag one or two peaks, marvelling at the terrific splendour of the Cuillin before dropping back down again into more comfortable terrain. However, the classic mountaineering challenge is to traverse the entire spine, taking in all twenty-two peaks, which amounts to a gruelling 10,000 feet (3,000 metres) of ascent. Add the walk-in (4 kilometres plus 900 metres of ascent) and walk out (5 kilometres and 960 metres of descent) and you are looking at a big day.

The first full traverse of the Ridge was done by Leslie Shadbolt and Alastair McLaren on 10 June 1911, who made it across in the remarkable time of 12 hours, 18 minutes. In 1928, Lilian Bray and sisters Sarah (known as Biddy) and Emily (known as Trilby) Wells from the Pinnacle Club completed the first all-women treverse. Since then, many thousands of scramblers, climbers and fell-runners have traipsed across, taking on the challenge at a variety of paces. Timing is integral to the challenge: with so much technical ground to cover, a certain timeliness is considered essential. Some carry bivi gear, adding an overnight camp on the Cuillin to reduce the pressure of the clock. Many do recce trips, familiarising themselves with the intricacies of sections of the Cuillin before finding a favourable day to race across, light and fast. Finlay Wild, a fell-runner and GP from Fort William, holds the current record for this style. In October 2013 he flew from Gars Bheinn to Sgùrr nan Gillean in a breathless 2 hours, 59 minutes, 22 seconds.

Like any diligent mountaineers, when I first came to the Cuillin with my friend Andy, we did our homework. From the shelter of Glen Brittle Youth Hostel, we consulted maps, checked weather forecasts and read up on the Ridge before embarking upon anything. All the guidebooks stressed the importance of recce trips, emphasising that the traverse was a formidable challenge, one not to be undertaken lightly, backing up that point with the remarkable statistic that 90 per cent of teams fail first time. Poring over the maps, struggling to pronounce the Gaelic names of the peaks, let alone memorise some of the ground we were bound to cover, we agreed that recce trips sounded wise, but we were pressed for time.

That week we had both taken leave from work and come

up north from Liverpool, stopping in Glencoe to take on some classic mountain challenges. We had tottered along the Aonach Eagach ridge and climbed the umpteen misty-damp pitches on Curved Ridge that led up to the summit of Buachaille Etive Mòr. There had been a few of the inevitable trying moments, but overall, things had gone well. Partnership is important in the mountains. With the wrong person, those routes could have been an ordeal but on these ventures Andy and I worked well together.

I liked heading into the mountains with Andy. A trainee doctor, he was not one of the macho whelps that went out looking for epics. He was by nature kind, fun and conscientious with an infectious zest for the Scottish hills, making him good company on a long tough day. Since he was older than me and had done his Mountain Leader qualification, he always seemed like a safe pair of hands. (It was only later that I found out that he had spent the previous week reading up on rope techniques, and so many of the systems we relied upon he had only just learned from a book.)

When we finally reached Skye, we had one final window – two more overcast July days – before we had to head back down south. Assuming that the Cuillin would be a longer version of the Aonach Eagach ridge, and with no time to find out whether that really was the case, we set out early one morning, tramping across the bog bound for the mighty Ridge, determined to give the traverse our best shot. Fortified by camaraderie, inexperience and youthful optimism, little did I realise quite what I was stumbling into.

———

Ahead, an impenetrable tower of broken black-brown blocks dominated the crest. We had reached Caisteal a' Gharbh-choire: Castle of the Rough Corrie. My mind reeled. Surely we wouldn't have to climb over this monster? I turned to Andy, who checked with the photocopied sheets of the guidebook.

'Looks like we drop down to the right here.'

'Righto.'

Dropping down off the ridge, feet padding carefully along rough-angled slabs and thin paths, we looked ahead, trying to decipher the line which would take us across the corrie bowl and back up onto the next wall of rocks, above which Sgùrr Dubh Mòr lurked unseen, lost inside a billowing cloud of vapour.

Some corries – the deep glacial bowls tucked into the hillside – are glorious, verdant hollows. In summer, these fertile folds fill with tussocks of sweet grass, offering a friendly bosom for grazers of the high mountains. Certain corries are the favoured nursing grounds of hinds, who gather in big herds to raise their calves inside the gentle enclaves. Before the Highland Clearances, when thousands of people were evicted from their home glens and islands, the lush corries were a vital component of the small-scale trans-humance farming culture of moving livestock up and down the hill according to the seasons. Every year, young women and men migrated uphill to stay in shielings (rough moun-tain dwellings) with their cattle, sheep and goats, which grazed the summer pastures on the common land. In Ireland, the same system was known as booleying, from *buaile*, a feeding or milking place for cows. The tradition was fondly recalled by those who could remember. For the young folk, the shieling or booleying season was a happy time of blessed freedom when the warm summer hillsides filled with music, laughter, dancing and flirting. (Perhaps the modern equivalent would be those teenage camping trips to fields, hills, woods, caves and music festivals?) Traces of that environmentally sensitive seasonal culture linger in place names, recorded on the maps. On the Cuillin the southernmost corries – Coire an Laogh, (Corrie of the Calf) and Coire a' Chruidh (Corrie of the Cattle) – may have been choice summer pastures.

But An Garbh-choire, the Rough Corrie, was not that sort of place. Greenery here was a thin line of grass, a surprise cushion of moss or a single Alpine flower, like lady's mantle, that nestled in a gravelly nook between sharp rocks.

The line across this tumultuous bowl of broken rocks was not clear and as we entered the corrie, things became more confused. The rocks grew and multiplied, demanding the most agile balancing and strenuous hauling to cross and leap from one individual to another, avoiding the forbidding black holes that appeared, everywhere, within this chaos of boulders beneath the Caisteal.

There was a very particular quality to these stones, unlike anything I had encountered elsewhere. Granite weathers into relaxed, round boulders. Running your hand over those crystalline forms, your palm might slide right around the piece, circumnavigating a whole rock, scarcely identifying any edge. Rhyolite forms more angular blocks which, with an irregular jumble of colours and textures, produces a mosaic effect that cries out to be explored by inquisitive hands and eyes. But the rocks in Garbh-choire did not welcome touch: they were savage and repellent.

By necessity, my hands reached out, fingers grasping at blocks to help pull and steady my hefty-rucksacked mass as I heaved through the tumbling corrie floor. But the rocks grabbed back, pinching, biting, snapping. Every boulder had jagged edges; every stone bristled; every surface within this stony field was covered in sharp abrasive points.

The Red Cuillin are formed from granite. The Black Cuillin is mostly gabbro: a dark, coarse-grained rock composed of interlocking, angular crystals. Place a toe on an edge or a boot on a slab: even if the surface is wet, the foot will stick, held in place by the most forceful friction. Climbers and mountaineers revel in this adhesive matter that formed around 60 million years ago, deep underground. The Cuillin rocks are the solidified remains of magma chambers that once fed active volcanoes set off by the opening of the north Atlantic, when tectonic plate movement pushed North America away from the UK. As well as the gabbros, the volcanism produced other rocks. Within the magma chamber, dykes and sills solidified into finer-grained sheets of rock. The notches, walls and blades that create the distinctive jagged outline of the Cuillin – features like the Inaccessible Pinnacle and the TD Gap – are formed of these intrusive basalts. Another geological aberration appears inside Garbh-choire. Those ultra-sharp ruddy-brown boulders that my younger self found so hard to handle are peridotite, a magmatic intrusion that is so rough it makes gabbro seem gentle.

—

Skirting under towering black buttresses, we circled the upper haunts of Coire a' Ghrunnda, hunting for a path that would lead us up through the gabbro quagmire and onto the summit of Sgùrr Alasdair.

But paths in the Cuillin bear little resemblance to paths elsewhere. As the terrain steepens, lines become faint or all but invisible. You approach an impenetrable mass of gabbro: which way to go? How to get around this sharp, bulging feature? Sometimes a thin line of trodden gravel appears, hugging the cliffs and skirting around precipices, but all routes must be approached with discerning caution. Some of the most obvious 'paths' lead to dizzying drops and impenetrable walls. Meeting such abrupt dead ends, you look around, but there is no other option and as you retrace your steps, you realise that this line is so well-trodden because many others before you have made this exact same mistake.

The gabbro does not help. Of the many minerals that comprise this rich, magmatic stone, there is one that upsets traditional navigation techniques. Magnetite, a black-grey mineral which is an oxide of iron, is magnetic. On the Cuillin, if you lay your compass down on the rocks, in some places the needle will spin, twirl and then settle into a mesmerising pendulum swing of 180°. A compass cannot be trusted on the Cuillin, since the rocks in these hills conjure their own magnetic field which overrides the pull of magnetic north.

Andy and I trudged on across the screes, but no path appeared. We kept going, conscious that having already made some navigational blunders in the Garbh-choire boulder field and on the clouded top of Sgùrr Dubh Mòr, we were behind schedule and needed to make up for lost time.

Eventually, we reached a point where the ground suddenly sheered away below us, dropping down an immeasurable height to another corrie far below. Struggling to read the gabbro labyrinth, we had missed the path and were once again off route: now facing the southwest ridge of Sgùrr Alasdair.

'What shall we do?' To my tired and inexperienced eyes, the ridge leading up to Sgùrr Alasdair looked to be a brutal mass of imposing rocky walls with horrific fall potential.

Andy was eyeing the ridge with a certain grim-faced resolution.

'I think I can see a way. I'll have to lead it.'

The rope and climbing equipment came out.

Andy moved slowly. Tense, tired hands and eyes scanned the rock faces – testing things out, feeling for a line up the steep-walled ridge. We were making progress: slow progress. Then he came to a stop.

He had followed the wall, cautiously moving up holds and ledges as they appeared, but here, things turned thin. He hunted around but there was no alternative. He faced a move: a delicate move; a strenuous move; a move that would send him momentarily out of balance. This was a move that in a bouldering gym he would pull off without thinking. But up here, there was no crash mat, no soft landing and no alternative.

Below us, cliffs, rocks and scree dropped sharply, tumbling through legions of vertical, gaping space. At Andy's back, his heavy rucksack tugged on his torso, opposing his intention, constantly pulling his body down towards gravity's outstretched arms.

'Watch me on this, Anna!'

'I'm watching!'

'What?!'

'I've got you!'

I stood on the belay, the rope held tight between my frantic fingers, willing him on, urging him to succeed, while time dilated on this stance at the edge of the world.

—

Stumbling up steep sharp rock after steep sharp rock; lungs gasping, heart pounding, legs burning; cursing Andy, cursing my rucksack, cursing the Cuillin – why was everything on this goddamn Ridge so goddamn hard? – I unexpectedly walked out into something special.

'Oh. Wow.'

'Sgùrr Alsadair!'

Andy stood nearby, grinning.

Rucksacks came off, banging down heavily on the summit at this natural stopping point. The big bags were a compromise. Having concluded that we were unlikely to pull off a speedy one-day traverse this time, we had packed enough kit to do it in two days. An overnight along the way, we reckoned, would buy us enough time to figure out the Cuillin as we went; however, the multi-day approach meant that we both had to carry more weight, with sleeping bag, roll mat, bivi bag and extra food added to the load. Perhaps if I had spent more time in cadets or done that Duke of Edinburgh award, I would have been better prepared to bear such a load, but as it was, my youthful body was struggling. Lugging that bag up and down the interminable peaks and troughs of the Cuillin was beginning to feel like a punishment of Sisyphean proportions.

But now – relieved of the bag and feeling blessedly light

– I turned on the spot, taking it all in. From up here, the
highest point on the Cuillin, we gazed down on the ridge
in all its terrible glory. The cloud had lifted and ahead and
behind stretched an epic spine of rocky peaks, crests and
pinnacles: a mesmerising high-line, falling away in searing
cliffs and plummeting screes down into the corries and out
into the bog, the islands and the ocean beyond.

As Andy took some photographs I tucked into a cereal
bar, only then realising I was hungry. Perhaps it was lunchtime? My mind and body had been so immersed in this
gruelling, complex terrain that it felt as though a lifetime
had passed, although maybe it was just a few hours. We still
had a long way to go.

'Bloody hell.'

'What?'

Looking up from his wrist, Andy's smile had slipped away.

'What is it?'

'It's gone three.'

Jesus.

We had been on the go for nearly nine hours and had
barely covered the first two kilometres of the ridge.

———

On the rock, time behaves very strangely. Personal clocks go
awry. Hunger, mood, alertness: internal cues vanish; their
voices lost to the screeching imperative of greater forces.

Immediate physical matter carries the utmost significance.
The block you stand on. The nut placed in a crack at your
feet. The fine edge around which your fingers curl, clasping
tight. The blank-looking wall above, which you scan, trying

to ascertain whether it has the features that you will need to stay on. With your whole being intent upon such physical immediacies, you lose touch with time and in that peculiar space, the present moment draws out – stretched open – pulled like elastic – bending and distorting time.

This warping of space and time completely threw me in my early climbing days. Again and again, I climbed, my whole being intent upon the intricacies of a small stretch of rock for what seemed like just a few minutes, but in reality, much more time had passed. Perhaps an hour; maybe two or three. Reading the rock, making decisions, summoning courage, committing to moves: each moment is so loaded with meaning. Whole days disappeared. Often – with a shock – hunger or darkness suddenly caught up with me, alerting me to the discordant passage of real time. I had no idea how long things took.

Time on rock can feel boundless, fathomless, infinite.

On that first venture of youthful optimism and inexperi-ence on the Cuillin, I stumbled into the most extreme geological disruption of time. Just as those rocks create their own magnetic field, overriding the standard pull of magnetic north, as I hauled myself across the gabbro, I came to learn that the Cuillin also has a startling propensity to engulf time.

—

Late afternoon. Tired. Hands, eyes, legs and feet had already navigated so much rock: so many tricky edges, tiny ledges, steep hauls and strenuous drops. And there was still so much to go.

Leaving Sgùrr Alasdair, we scrambled down off the peak,

avoiding the gaping cleft where a thousand-foot cascade of scree plummeted down to the corrie far below in a remarkable feature known as the Great Stone Chute. Instead of descending, we tackled yet another tricky scramble, taking on yet more difficult steps, boots wedged onto tenuous edges, hands clinging to features as I pulled my heavy mass up a steep wall of gabbro, my rucksack weighing heavier as the day wore on, constantly threatening to pull me off balance.

From the top of Sgùrr Thearlaich, we teetered down a bizarre sequence of slabby gabbro panels in a disconcerting trust exercise. Feet flat, knees bent, thighs straining to maintain my mass within the right spot to pull off this sequence of angled-balanced-friction movements.

After the slabs, a run of lumpy ledges leading down the eastern face of the ridge, all falling away sharply into yet another distant corrie – Coir' an Lochain – where a pool of water sat in the green opening far below. Turning into the Cuillin to steady myself, I tried to disregard the great space opening out all around me.

Two hands wrapped around a great rough chunk of gabbro, two feet seeking out positive ledges below to drop down onto, I leaned into the rock, fighting the pull of the rucksack, when suddenly – awfully – the entire block reared backwards out of the mountain.

A savage drop below.

A great weight on my back.

Nothing to break my fall.

Nothing to grab.

Lost to gravity and gabbro, I fell backwards into that horrific falling feeling – the free fall that precedes the crash – but then something caught. With a sharp lurch, the knot on my harness pulled tight and the rope took my weight as the rock crashed down through my legs, glancing off an ankle, tearing free in a mesmerising splay of power. Thundering downhill, the roar of rockfall boomed out across the corrie and up onto the ridge as the rock wheeled through scree and crashed over boulders before splitting apart in a terminal burst of explosive fragmentation. A line of white dust trailed across the debris and, rising acrid up the hillside, came the explosive stench of gunpowder.

We regrouped. I sat down heavy and stared out across Loch Coruisk, the Red Cuillin and Blà Bheinn, completely indifferent to their majestic forms, as I returned from the brink of a mortal abyss.

In my tired inexperience, I had made a devastating mistake. I hadn't tested the block. I hadn't kicked or shaken it, checking for movement. Instead, I had simply trusted, clung and hung. And so when that rock came loose – the entire rock upon which my whole life at that moment depended – I was utterly done for. But for Andy. Andy had saved my life. He had had me on a short rope, and when my rock tore loose, he held me, anchored to a boulder above.

Exhausted, wrung out, shaken, shocked: that whole long day had been such hard physical and mental work. All day we had been hauling up tough rocks, edging over treacherous ground, figuring out perplexing navigation, getting things wrong and having to redress mistakes; all of which played out within the eye of constant searing exposure. And now this. I was at my limit. I could feel tears, fear and panic rising within – a violent emotional reaction to a thunderous incident.

But we still had so much ground to cover: so many more

tricky edges, ledges, airy steps and long, loose, sliding slopes before we reached anything that bore any semblance to the safe horizontal world. And so, as shock shook my core, pushing me towards a vortex of rock-induced high emotion, I pushed back.

Not now, Anna. This. Is. Not. The. Time. Not now.

I got to my feet, breathing slow and deep, and began again, taking steady steps on my battered ankle, letting the reverberations of that cataclysmic moment settle through movement.

———

Our route led us on through a sharp cleft and out onto Collie's Ledge, a thin line that crosses a sheer rocky face high above Coire Lagan, where Andy marvelled at the exposure and I hobbled along, somewhat less effusive. Climbing back upon ourselves, we reached the summit of Sgùrr Mhic Chòinnich, our third and final top. From here, the only way was down.

Turning away from the Inaccessible Pinnacle, we tumbled down An Stac screes, stumbling out into the base of Coire Lagan where I wobbled on my shattered legs like a newborn calf. After such an extended intensive period on the rocks, I had become grey, hard and stony but, finally, ahead lay the most glorious prospect. Grass, moss and a lochan full of water – soft, green, living liquid matter – startling my gravelled eyes, easing me back into another state of being.

All around the corrie little stone circles and oblongs appeared, tucked between boulders, like the ones I had encountered on the Ridge, a lifetime ago, on the way up to

Sgùrr nan Eag. What had seemed horrendous up there now appeared positively homely. Selecting a welcoming stone-fold sanctuary, we laid out our sleeping bags, heated water and cooked tea, the warm food settling our hungry stomachs, and we were soon set for the night. Here, at last, my exhausted body could rest.

Sleeping on a mountain can be such a peculiar experience. There you are, high up in the world, out in the open air among grasses, mosses, lichens and rocks, encircled by epic geological forms shaped by times and processes well beyond your comprehension, and there – as you pass on into the liminal space between sleep and wakefulness, as mind and body relax and drift – things make sense. The breath settles, gradually deepening, the chest rising and falling, as your being mingles into the great, breathing mountain world.

That night was one of the strangest mountain sleeps I have ever had. The Cuillin, which swallowed so much time and energy through the day, now stole into our sleep, weaving its own mysterious spell there. Tucked inside that little gabbro fold beside tiny yellow stars of tormentil, the healing flower, our aching minds and limbs warmed, relaxed and fell into bewitched slumbers.

Clouds came and went. Light drizzle fell. Stars pivoted across the sky. Satellites passed. Perhaps the moon rose and set.

I don't know. We slept.

And slept.

And slept.

After giving everything to the Cuillin for thirteen long hours, that night, we were lost on the Cuillin for another thirteen hours.

Thirteen hours to cover less than a third of the ridge followed by thirteen hours lying comatose on the mountain. When we finally woke, we packed up and trudged out. I had had my epic and did not come away fortified with a breezy story. Our time on the Cuillin gave me a new appreciation of the scale of technical and physical challenge one could meet in the mountain environment. I walked away feeling deeply humbled, carrying an enhanced respect for the gravity of these heightened places.

V

LAKE DISTRICT

RHYOLITE

Climbing is not a sport: it's a way of life.

– Bill Birkett

One damp Tuesday in July, I stomped up and over the fells from Grasmere into Langdale. Sometimes, Grasmere – with all its daffodils, dead poets and rain-darkened slate buildings – could feel terribly claustrophobic. I never tired of Langdale. I always loved the point where, coming over the top, the sky opened out and I could peer into the U-shaped trough of Great Langdale. I never quite knew what I would find. The weather in the Lakes is so particular. One valley might be dank and misty, with a light rain falling, while the next might be dry. At the head of Langdale, sometimes Crinkle Crags, Bowfell and the Langdale Pikes cut sharp, forbidding silhouettes. Sometimes banks of dark cloud sit heavy over the peaks and glaring white lines pour down the fells. Wisps of white cloud might blow across the group, gathering in folds and spilling over edges. In mizzle, the peaks vanish and the head of the valley fills with light.

That particular Tuesday was warm and damp and beneath the overcast sky, the fells wore a rich, saturated summer green.

On the steep drop into Langdale, I stopped at a rock. It was a good stone, the kind dropped by a retreating glacier perhaps. Large, bald, flat-topped, grey-coloured with little white, blue and green lichen splodges, it made an ideal lunch stone. Rummaging through my bag to locate my sandwiches, I looked up and jumped. A little creature had slid over to join me and it now lay curled across a stone at my feet. The width of my finger, its brassy body was the length of a good stick ruler and with two gleaming black bug eyes, this was no snake. It was a slow worm that had silently appeared, perhaps like me, venturing out to its own chosen rock in the hope that the sun would come out too. (It didn't. That day was warm, overcast and damp. Good weather for slugs, who were out in force.) As I munched my sandwiches and looked across the brackened fells, I also glanced down from time to time, checking in with my companion. One of the joys of going out alone is that it makes you more open to encounters with other beings. Whether people, plants, rocks, birds, beasts, insects or elements, I love a chance meeting – the stranger the better.

The slow worm was a quiet fellow, seemingly content to recline, without moving, atop its own stone, but such repose was not for me. I had other places to be.

Bidding the beast adieu, I continued my journey, brushing on through damp bracken and tall pink foxgloves, bound for my chosen rocks. Eventually I reached the spot where a weathered purple buttress tumbled out of the hillside. Bays of juniper, holly and rowan grew at the foot of the crag, interrupting the rock form – higher up, the vegetation became sparse until there was nothing but rock stretching up towards the skyline.

With a shiver of excitement, I ditched my rucksack and unlaced my heavy-soled leather boots, replacing them with thin rubber climbing shoes. No rope, no harness, no gear, no partner. Freedom and anticipation swirled, giddy and intoxicating.

Suddenly, I felt very light.

The challenge, with soloing, is to stay calm and focused. Climbing without a rope or partner, there is no backup. The higher you climb, the further you risk falling. No wobbles. No doubts. No panic.

Stay cool.

Stepping up to Scout Crag, I placed my hands on the stone; ready to find my way.

As my feet made their first tentative moves off the ground, the rock rose to meet me. Cautiously moving up into the grooves, little by little, I found the stone was remarkably detailed. Among the ramps, blocks and arêtes, holds, edges, corners and flakes appeared, everywhere, welcoming my fingers. There were damp patches – seeping cracks and sodden black moss – but with care, they could be avoided.

If walking alone increases your sensitivity to the environment, soloing does the same, but more so. Without a rope or a partner, senses turn super-heightened. I pay extra-close attention to the surfaces around me, picking up the details and placing my limbs with the utmost precision. Sounds come in, sharp: from distant noises – sheep calling, a dog barking, a shepherd blaspheming – to the sound of my own breath and heartbeat. The key is to absorb all of the necessary information without getting overwhelmed or distracted. To stay focused, listening, observing, moving and relaxing.

On Upper Scout Crag, the rock was rough, pocked and

grippy. Everything was there and things fell into place. Inside the rhyolite collage, I stretched and folded and clasped, becoming plastic – feet, legs, arms and hips all moving together with the rock – relishing the shapes the rhyolite drew out of mind, muscle and sinew.

The routes were long – thirty, fifty metres – and with such lengthy sequences something switched. Fear did not increase with height. Instead, the further I climbed, the more I relaxed and floated, letting the rock stream carry me up and away.

———

In 2015, I landed in the centre of the mosaic of mountain environment, culture and tourism that is the Lake District. My research project included a year-long placement at the former home of William and Dorothy Wordsworth – Dove Cottage, now a museum and archive just outside the village of Grasmere. Relocating there was no great hardship. Since discovering the fells during my undergraduate days in Liverpool, I had been coming up to the Lake District on a regular basis with various groups of friends.

I loved the freedom, escape and boisterous physical fun that came with each of those visits to the Lakes. We camped and climbed, swam and scrambled, embracing the many raw features of that northern glacial landscape. But on those short trips, I was conscious that I was a visitor; a weekend warrior, taking in the national park through brief snatches of exotic experience, which was far from the full picture. I wanted more. I wanted to know what it was like to live in that place week after week. I wanted the local perspective;

the lived experience. I wanted to grasp the rough texture that lay beneath the veneer of art, culture and holiday. Living in the Lakes, I soon came to see things differently.

I arrived in January, when it was cold, dark and wet. Sleet and hail came in and the snow line moved up and down the fells, occasionally shining brightly on clear winter days. This was not climbing weather, but still I went out often alone, pacing the home range. There was little else to do and besides, I was curious. Circling the local lakes of Rydal and Grasmere, I met the geese and oystercatchers. Pacing up onto White Moss Common, sometimes I startled a deer or a crew of stout-legged Herdwicks busy munching. In the woods at Baneriggs and Red Bank I might glimpse red squirrels springing through the moss and leaf litter. Then, ranging up onto the fells, I took in the higher points of Alcock Tarn, Stone Arthur, Helm Crag, Silver How and Loughrigg Fell – places where occasional trees grew in crazy precarious positions. Leaning out of rocky outcrops, the junipers, yews, rowans and hollies hung onto gaps in the vertical ground, finding enclaves just out of reach of the hungry grazers.

At first, going out after work meant walking in the dark, which I liked. I rarely took a torch. I liked getting away from the glare of cars, screens and street lamps and letting my senses adjust to the gloom, noting how my hearing heightened in the darkness, how my ears tuned into sounds in a way they never would in the daylight. A rustle in the undergrowth and everything stopped – heart, breath – listening deeply until the instincts unwound and reason cut in, reminding me that there was no danger in this place.

As the days lengthened, the village got busier. Cars and coaches streamed in and out – visitors thronged on the pavements and footpaths – and yet their schedule was fairly predictable. By 6 p.m. most had retreated indoors and the fells fell quiet. Keeping up my nightwalking, setting out to join the bats and badgers, I found my breathing space.

It did not take long for this compulsive roaming to alter my grasp of the place. As a visitor, I had previously relied on daylight hours and Ordnance Survey maps to navigate the fells. Then I stuck to the path networks and stopped frequently to check features against map symbols, which made my trips out something of a stop-start orienteering exercise, performed in dialogue with the paper authority: the map. But as a resident, those flat sheets soon became redundant. The lines that I was tracing over and over again enabled me to build my own map. Straying off the twilight paths, I clambered over walls and fences, rummaging through woods and following becks where I might discover hidden plunge pools and old mines. Pacing out the hollows and contours, uncovering secret pockets, my legs soon fashioned a new muscular familiarity with the landscape, gradually connecting the dots, reaching towards a comprehensive and lived knowledge of the landscape.

Living in the central fells paved the way for a different relationship to landscape and climbing than I had known before. Unlike my prior visits to rock country – trips out to north Wales, the Peak District, Wharfedale, Skye or Kalymnos – inside the fells, I was immersed in rock. The stones were everywhere. They were in the houses and barns, stone walls and footpaths. They burst from the ground in outcrops and boulders, they poured down the fells in cliffs and crags and they sat in piles, heaped up into cairns to mark the summits. As I settled into life in Grasmere, I began to see how the rocky terrain runs through the people who live in those places.

Along with roaming the fells, working in the museum, researching and climbing, I also gave a significant portion of my time that year to another local institution. This one had flagstone floors, a blazing fire and a line of taps connected to an often-changed set of barrels. Like the many pubs across the Lake District, my local, Tweedies, was a fine establishment.

Midweek the bar was quiet but at the weekends tides of visitors poured in, clamouring for drinks and gourmet meals, and so my clan of lower-income museum colleagues ended up pushed into a corner where we rubbed up against another crew of locals – *local* locals, Cumbrians born and bred. Initially they were reticent and a little stand-offish but once they warmed up, the stories flowed, illuminating a Cumbria that was worlds apart from the visitor experience.

From the corners of several favourite pubs, these men drank, chatted and observed the endless flow of Gore-Tex-clad visitors with bemused indifference. When yet another exhibitionist in an expensive jacket showed up rattling his climbing wares, they rolled their eyes without comment. They had seen it all before. They were hard as nails, but were not braggers. They were subversives, of a kind.

Wrestling crag-fast sheep off godforsaken vegetated ledges, secret raves in hidden mines or the unexplained disappearance of a bike chain on a late-night cycle home – such stories were all part of the repertoire. One had a particularly entertaining tale of disrupting a local fox hunt. While the sportsmen tried to locate their prey, communicating via walkie-talkie, this guy tapped the line, keeping them off the scent by shouting mixed messages and confused directions into the frequency.

They were always out and about and so they duly showed up in the pub with some fresh tale of where they had been and what they seen. By day they were stonemasons, path-builders and wallers, in the evenings and at weekends they climbed, walked, cycled and scrambled. Their knowledge of their home fells and valleys ran broad and deep and yet there was always something new to explore – some ghyll to clamber, a cliff to investigate or a bird sighting to chase up. Unlike other outdoorsy types, they never spoke of kit or technique. Conversation centred on people, places and history, or plants, birds and animals. Their interest was the environment – their home environment – which they sought to know in all of its aspects and layers. I had never met outdoors folk quite like them. In their company, I began to see climbing in a new light.

———

The rock helped. There was something about rhyolite – the dominant rock of the fells – that spoke to me. This stone, fired into existence some 450 million years ago, speaks to another Lake District. Unlike the balanced, harmonious landscape of the present, celebrated by so many painters, poets and other romantic souls, the Borrowdale Volcanic Group formed when tectonic plates were shifting and colliding, forcing one beneath another, causing the mantle, deep beneath the surface, to melt. Earth erupted. Sticky lava and fountains of fluid lava surged from vents and craters. Pyroclastic flows of rock, ash and hot gases ripped through the landscape over the course of many explosive eruptions. This ejecta material is still present in the fells: the finer ash formed tuff; the larger matter became agglomerate. The igneous rocks – andesite, basalt and rhyolite – are compositional varieties of the magma that erupted. The result of all of this tectonic-volcanic activity is incredible diversity within the present-day Lakeland rocks.

Rhyolite weathers into features that make for instinctive climbing. Little cracks, slots and pockets line the faces, welcoming fingers, toes and gear. Along with these openings, protrusions also burst out from the crags, forming edges and ledges where you can stop and comfortably belay in the company of a holly or rowan tree. The jagged erosion style also gives rise to blocks, flakes and pinnacles – rising into sharp triangles like teeth or shark fins – points of interest to handle or wrestle, depending on their outlook.

In contrast to gritstone, where the colour range is so limited that the crags resemble pieces from Picasso's brown phase, rhyolite rocks are more like Impressionist paintings. Up close, you see past the broad grey edifice and find that the surface is animated with strokes of colour. Little Chamonix, a popular route on Shepherd's Crag in the Borrowdale oakwoods, holds a remarkable sequence of colours.

Starting in the grey corner, I moved upwards, leaving behind the ferns and brambles to swing out – the air opening in a sudden position of great exposure – but there was a red flake to grasp, toes pushing down on a nerve-wrackingly worn stone nipple, and then I had topped up and out, breathing more freely in a leafy green oak bay. But this was far from the end. Little Chamonix has several pitches. Next comes the enigma. Inside a Byzantine corner, a polished plate of soapy blue stone awaits. I moved up, bum-sliding across the plate, wondering how to make it off again. Looking across an expanse of air, my eyes located the following steps. A couple of chinks stand out like milky-blue cataracts on an otherwise smooth purple-grey slab – I breathed in and leaned across – moving out of balance – hoping and trusting the cataracts would hold as I toppled into a new balance. They held and the next few moves saw me out onto a new face, leaning into a pocked orange pinnacle where I stopped, breathing heavily into that pointillist surface, marvelling at the many grains of weathered mineral colour.

As well as soaking up the intricate details of the climbs, with repeat visits to a range of local outcrops, I came to see how the crags are part of the life of the valleys. On Raven Crag above Walthwaite, sounds from Elterwater and Chapel Stile drift up to the rock face. Sheep bleat. Cars and Land Rovers pass along the narrow, walled lane. Chattering walkers and barking dogs traipse up and down the paths. On the hour, every hour, the church clock sounds and from the slate quarry come alarms, bleeping vehicles and occasional blasts. This crag, like so many other exposed rock faces, acts like a giant ear, listening in to the many voices of Langdale life.

Those purple-tinged rocks also offer a great perspective on the valley. Climbing up the face beside the yew trees, pausing on ledges lined with aspens, or belaying from the top, we looked back from time to time. From those perched vantage points, we might watch vehicles circling the blue-grey slate quarry pit or observe the coppiced woodland that softened this open end of Langdale – a reminder of the not-too-distant past when this part of the valley hosted a thriving gunpowder industry.

Tuning into and out of the rocks, watching and listening through the simple act of spending time at crags like this, enables a distinct type of place-knowing. Being present in this way, a climber becomes party to the ambience of a place. A crag can thus provide a window on the life and rhythms of a place, situating the climber as both observer and participant.

Bramcrag Quarry is another distinctive crag which puts the climber in touch with an alternative aspect of the Lake District. To reach these quarried rocks, we wandered in up the old trackway from St John's in the Vale, passing through the plantation pines and breaking out onto the upper rubble slopes where open flower banks emerged. Ragwort, foxgloves, yellow peas, purple heather and clover – the weeds were prolific and beautiful. Then we paced along a stone causeway elevated over scenes of industry past and present. Below us lay rusting hulks and old vehicles, sheds, containers, tramlines and stacks of timber, since the crypt-like space at the base of the quarry now served as a timber yard.

The climbing takes place on an igneous intrusion of fine-grained microgranite. On the long slab lines like Fargo, Sunburst Slab and Blencathra Badger I set off, armed with a clutch of quickdraws which I would pause to clip onto the metal bolts, connecting the rope to the rock to keep me safe as I climbed higher. I moved eagerly up those walls, excited to pull out the choreography that lay hidden within the bumping, rippling slabs. Bounding, bouncing, padding, balancing – reaching, grasping and releasing – passing between bays of gorse, heather, fern and rosebay willow herb, each thirty-metre line held me captivated, caught up in the measured flow of rhythmic stone sequencing. The steeper lines of Morley Street Mission, the Quarryman and Last Dash demanded a more fiery physicality. Committing to those burly routes meant pulling up hard into sharp-flaked corners; hands clamped tight around blocky pieces; arms and legs burning with the spate of strong movements.

Beyond the rusting industrial matter, views opened out across river meadows and rolling hay fields above which the shapely mountain fells of Skiddaw and Blencathra slowly mellowed in the setting sun. A kestrel might circle over, surveying the terrain, stopping to hover, wings beating, before the creature relaxed, released and moved on. We went in the evenings, when the timber yard was quiet. Sometimes we climbed alone and sometimes we shared the stone panels with nuclear engineers. Old meets new, industrial-pastoral – it was a strange place to climb, a brilliant intrusion, disrupting the well-rehearsed and sometimes overly polished idyll of the Lake District brand.

———

The valley crags and their cragsmen thus encouraged me, pushing me on to gain greater skill at handling the rock and, as my craft improved, my eyes began to roam higher. The fells captivated me. Whenever I had the chance, my walking legs carried me up those steep hillsides, following the stony paths or picking my own line through the rocks, grasses, bracken and mosses, to head up into the heights. Sometimes I entered dismal grey cloud and traipsed on, against all reason, suffering at the hands of the bleak, cold and wet mountain environment. On better days, leaving the valley behind, new horizons emerged. I might catch a glimpse of Barrow shipyard and Blackpool Tower to the southwest, or Ingleborough and the Yorkshire Dales to the east. I began to recognise the fells by their distinctive shapes. The triangle of Wetherlam, the point of Old Man of Coniston, Crinkle Crags and Bowfell, the Langdale Pikes and the long line of High Street. Up in the heights, I found a community of hills and as my climbing improved, a new desire emerged. The urge to link these two worlds: the mountain and the rock climb.

My first proper attempt began at Honister Pass with Will. We had a big scheme in mind. We were bound for Grey Knotts, where we would drop down a gully and climb Gillercombe Buttress, a seven-pitch route weaving up a south-facing mountain crag. This was a big route, coupled with a reasonable walk-in through the fells, but that was not all we had our sights on that day. Once we had finished that climb, we planned to hike onwards to another mountain crag where we would take on a couple more routes – Sledgate Ridge and Engineer's Slabs – from which we would top out onto the summit of Great Gable.

Groaning under the weight of climbing bags, we left the car behind and began the trudge uphill. This was not like those evenings where I danced across the fells, carrying only the weight of myself. Lugging all the climbing gear – the ropes and rack, the food and spare layers – made the walk-in onerous. We sweated and panted, calf muscles complaining. To climb in the mountains, you had to really want it.

One step at a time, pace by pace, we gradually left the road behind, rising up away from the old slate mine, moving into the higher domain where we met rusting wire fences, rocky cairns and flowering grasses.

'Here?'

We peered down a gully – a long steep chute of damp sludge, plants and gravel – a rough line of weakness that would lead us off the top and down to the foot of the crag that we intended to climb.

'Yep. Let's do it.'

Down, down, down. Feet sliding and slipping in the loose matter. Hands grasping at rocks or tufts of vegetation – we sprackled and tumbled, moving with gravity while trying to hold something back. Descent has its own treachery. Finally, we stumbled out of the bottom and headed out on more level ground, hunting for the start of our route.

Finding a climb can be surprisingly difficult. Routes are rarely signposted, since traditional ethics dictate that we should leave the rock as we find it. (This is why bolting and even chalk use can cause controversy.) With no obvious indicators, is easy to look at a crag and see a maze of rock and grassy ledges – then, blinded by the mass of information, eyes scan left to right, up and down, failing to light upon anything useful. Sometimes you approach the crag with a clearer idea, an image of what you think you should find, but this can also cause problems. It is easy to imagine features in the shape that you desire and so you set off on the route you think you should be on but then, some way down the line, nagging doubts set in and you realise you are on a red herring, journeying into unknowns and impassabilities.

Skirting around the foot of the buttress, we picked up a faint trail. Marking the rock is frowned upon, but still climbers leave little signs. Like an animal tracker, when hunting for a route on a mountain crag I tune into the vegetation. I note where the grass is trampled and worn into paths, observing where these lines go, looking out for the slightly bigger compressions which could mark the stance at the bottom of a route.

'Here!'

Trampled grass and a passage of rock where the edges had a dull sheen, suggesting the movement of prior hands and feet. We had found the start of Gillercombe Buttress. Out came the rope and gear, helmets and harnesses and we were soon away, climbing into the many aspects of the mountain crag.

We alternated leads, pitching up through fluid sequences of stony steps, edges and corners, running into occasional technical sections where the feet went high, placed with precision, while the arms stretched higher still, reaching with hope, lighting on something solid to pull up on as the rocks provided the shapes we needed to move up the steep ground.

In this focused partnership dance, height came as a surprise. Pausing on belay ledges, once the anchors were set, I looked out, astonished to see the space opening all around us. Below us lay a great mossy bowl where water gleamed in rills, gathering into a gill that tumbled down, out of sight, into the lower pastures of Seathwaite. The rock face seemed like a great vertical stage overlooking a vast mountain amphitheatre. In this big arena, the flow of gravity seemed to reverse, as though the midsummer updraught were lifting us like thistledown, floating us up the rock face, back up into the heightened realm of light, air, stone and ruffled grass.

Topping out, exhilarated, we slumped on the rounded slopes of Grey Knotts, lying among the soft mosses, eating and drinking and laughing, replenishing ourselves ready to continue on to the next part of the journey. Great Gable was waiting.

On the fell-top traverse to our next climb, we passed walkers. So many walkers – so many people out with family and friends, roaming freely through the fells. Stone Cove, the high hollow between Great Gable and Green Gable, was busy. People were rattling down the red screes from Windy Gap, trudging wearily up the beck from Ennerdale and a number of black dots swept along the skyline. Crossing the beck, we left the paths, picking our own line up through a broken boulder field to reach the shadowed north face. There was no one on this part of the mountain.

As we gained ground, the cliff grew, becoming an imposing and complex face. This was not one of those sheer cliffs where sheets of rock gleamed, uninterrupted. There was a lot of greenery about. Grassy ledges and banks appeared everywhere among the rock, interrupting the stone flow – but still, we could see some promise. In among the shadowed plants we saw coloured walls and textured slabs; cracks, corners and blocks; a feast of intrigue and challenge, leading right up to the summit plateau of one of the highest tops in England.

We found the crack at the start of Sledgate Ridge and Will headed up the steep line to a green ledge. He puffed and panted, relishing the strain, moving, as usual, with bold strength. But when he reached an easy angled slab – ground that he would normally dart across – he hesitated. Then stopped.

Black debris began raining down the rock face, accompanied by a great stream of expletives. He began moving again, slowly. More black matter came down. More swearing.

The problem, I soon found, was moss. Everywhere. Chunks and pillows and little black tendrils grew all over the rock face. Holds were hidden. Stances unclear. Fingers and toes struggled for purchase. Grabbing at an edge, the surface shifted, as the gritty matter intervened between skin and rock. The grime clung to hands and feet. Again and again I wiped them clean, stopping on edges, perching like a flamingo, balanced on one leg to rub the toes of my shoes against the inside of the opposite trouser leg. I never knew moss could make climbing so difficult.

'This is horrible!'

'I know! Keep going!'

On lead, my nut key became invaluable. I was used to using the hooked end of this thin metal tool to lever wedged gear out of clean cracks. But up here, the cracks were full of crud. Before I could even start the process of rattling through my gear and deciding which piece to place, I had to run the key through the rock slot, scooping out reams of black earthy matter to open a cavity for protection.

I had heard climbers complain about dirty routes before. On Yorkshire gritstone this meant slimy green chimneys and ledges full of bird shit. But this was my first proper brush with 'gardening': a term used with disdain to describe the ordeal of climbing archaic routes, where the geology is obscured beneath a myriad of vegetable life. Our climb up the north face of Great Gable was suggesting that far from a pinnacle of sublime experience, rock climbing on a mountain could be hard, slow, dirty work.

As I diligently scraped and cleaned, working awkwardly with this wild garden of a rock climb, I was reminded of an old story about Lakeland climbing – that some of the crags here had been excavated by climbers. At some point in the last century, there had been a hunger for new rock, leading to an industrious phase of turning out new crags where crags had never been before by burning off plants and digging out walls. Was this one of those crags? Had Gable reclaimed its rocks?

After digging out my own anchor, temporarily securing myself to the rock face, I tried to relax, letting my thoughts wander off the convoluted mess of moss, rock, rope and grime we had fumbled our way into. Peering around, I hunted for something more banal or tranquil to settle on, but there was nothing moderate about our situation. Unlike the hanging valley that held Gillercombe Buttress, this shady north face looked out over reams of unbroken space. My vision flowed out, swooping along the sweeping glacial trough of Ennerdale. A solitary youth hostel sat above dark conifer plantations.

Towering over the valley, there was Pillar Rock, another lofty outcrop that can only be reached by climbing. The first to do this was a shepherd named John Atkinson, who made it to the top in 1826, performing one of the earliest recorded rock climbs in the Lake District. In subsequent years, that exposed mountain rock went on to become a bustling climbing venue, frequented by crowds of traditional climbers out with hemp ropes and hobnailed boots, but fashions change. Now mountain cragging, with the big walk-in and long committing adventure, doesn't have the appeal that it once had. I pictured the routes on Pillar – high and dramatic; polished and mossy – a tribute to a bygone climbing era.

Then I noticed a change on the horizon. Cloud was blowing in from the Irish Sea and the top of Pillar was disappearing inside a mass of swirling vapours. I tried to recall what the forecast had said. Was it supposed to rain? It was one thing climbing on this exposed, perplexing mossy line when the rocks were dry, but to climb up here, when these sinister stones disappeared inside a thicket of damp cloud, or worse still – rain or thunder – that would be horrific. My heart raced. *Climb faster.*

The third pitch led us up a bruised corner of purple rhyolite. Reaching around the pillars and edges, feet balancing and bridging, we finally left the moss behind, at last grasping some good handfuls of rough stone. But by this point, swinging up the steepening wall towards a perched block that hung ominously on the skyline, I had had enough. Enough of the finely balanced finger, toe and body work. Enough of the exposed lofty landscape. I wanted some solid ground beneath my feet.

From the top of Sledgate Ridge, we looked across to the neighbouring wall. There was Engineer's Slabs, the third and final route of our scheme, a remote line that would lead us up a brilliant piece of mountain rock, topping out onto the peak. But, tired, chilled and slightly spooked, we were in no state to continue. Our travail up this atmospheric enclave had left heads and bodies spangled.

Fumbling on, we made for the safety of the summit via a sketchy zig-zag up broken walls, bumbling over treacherous ledges. The foliage thickened. Deep spongy carpets of moss, slippery tufts of grass and dense banks of great wood-rush lined every edge. Grabbing handfuls of those tough stems, hoping they would hold, we gambolled up and on, watching for loose rock, feet sinking and sliding as we cut our escape route through the vertical jungle. Finally, the angle eased, the forest diminished and we emerged, dazed, onto the bald summit plateau of Great Gable.

The transition was abrupt.

On this large sweep of level ground, walkers casually strolled to and from the summit block, chatting, snacking and taking photos. Up here, on this summer afternoon, Great Gable was balmy – hard to conceive that just a few metres away lay an entirely different experience. Wild-eyed, helmets on heads, gear rattling from our harnesses, it seemed as though we had dropped in from another planet. Now, with the whole sole making steady contact with the level ground, finally, nerves began to relax.

I had always looked on Great Gable as a benign fell. Unlike its more sinister neighbour Scafell, the highest mountain in England, which often lurks beneath a forbidding shroud of mist and cloud, Great Gable seemed a relatively amiable mountain. Each of my prior ventures up onto that top had affirmed that feeling. Walking up Gable was an easy pleasure, a matter of pacing up the paths, winding through the grasses and stones, coming in and out of the clouds that might mass around the tops. But Gable was a mountain with a secret. Rock climbing on the north face had revealed that, like Jekyll and Hyde, beyond the bald stony summit and the easy grassy slopes, the familiar mountain had a darker, wilder side.

—

On some Friday night or other in Tweedies when – third or fourth pint in hand – I was prattling on about how much I loved the sport of climbing, one of the locals brought me up short.

'Climbing is not a sport: it's a way of life.'

This reprimand was delivered by Bill Birkett. As with most things in my early climbing days, I didn't really know who he was until I mentioned him to Carl.

'Bloody hell, Bill Birkett?! He's a proper legend – we've got a stack of his books at home!'

Bill, it turned out, was a climber and writer from Langdale. In typical Cumbrian fashion, he was reticent about his past attainments, but once I found out his initials were T.W., I found his name attached to many hard routes across the Lake District. He had been a very strong climber in the 1970s and 1980s – but there was more to it than this. Another wild-haired and weather-beaten guy who sometimes showed up in the pub was his nephew Dave Birkett, another cutting-edge climber from Langdale.

Dave had picked up where Bill left off, putting up new climbs across the UK that were so difficult I could scarcely dream of what the climbing entailed, although his evocative route names helped. There was Skye Wall (E7 6b), Dawes Ridges a Shovelhead (E8 6c), Once Upon a Time in the South West (E9 6c) and on Scafell's ominous East Buttress, Return of the King (E9 6c). Along with Dave, there was his wife, Mary Birkett, another formidable climber, and the latest arrival on the scene was Will Birkett, Bill's son, who looked set to continue the family tradition. The Birketts, I soon learned, were a local climbing dynasty.

The line started with Bill's dad, Jim. Born in Little Langdale in 1914, Jim Birkett was a pioneer in many senses. He left school at fourteen to start as an apprentice slate river at a local quarry.[16] Later, he went on to work at Honister and Moss Rig Quarry. When Jim took to the rocks in the

1940s, neither locals nor working-class people climbed. Climbing was a pursuit for wealthier visitors. Locals watched on as they poured into Langdale on motorbikes with ropes strung around their shoulders.

Entering the world of gentlemen climbers could be daunting for a working man. Snobbery was rife. Bill Peascod, a coal miner and contemporary of Jim Birkett from west Cumbria, reflected that he and Jim were among the first working-class people to make an impact on the British climbing scene. 'Although I longed to be part of the climbing fraternity, I was ashamed to be a coal miner; when I mixed with other climbers I used to hide the fact, attempt to put on a cultured accent and keep my coal-blackened fingernails out of sight.'[17] The answer, for Peascod, 'was to climb harder and better than anyone else. Climb so hard they had to sit up and notice us.'[18] Whether it's class, gender, race, faith or sexuality, for a minority – any minority – entering a field that is dominated by another group is arduous. To be equal, you have to be better. Jim managed that. Over a ten-year period, he put up nearly fifty of the highest standard routes across the Lakes, concluding in 1949 with Harlot Face (E1), one of the hardest climbs in Britain at that time.

The quarryman thus made it into the history books – but never told his son. Bill only found out that his father had been a climber when he took to the rocks in his late teens and discovered, time and time again, his father's name attached to so many great routes.

As I became more familiar with Bill and his family, I was struck not so much by their elite abilities, but the way that their climbing prowess was folded into a particular way of life. Rock is their medium. Living locally, these climbing craftsmen all work the stone – first Jim as a slate quarryman and now Dave and Will as stonemasons. Monday to Friday they dress the rocks, constructing walls and buildings across their home valleys, reshaping the area's stony architecture. And their skilful approach widens out into environmentalism. When Jim stopped climbing, he continued using his expertise as a volunteer for the Nature Conservancy, clambering up cliffs and insecure steep ground to check bird nests. Similarly, Dave rescues stranded sheep and works to protect the endangered red squirrel population.

Heading out to climb with Bill, he always pointed out the world around the rock. He knew the routes, personalities and histories of the local climbers and also spoke fluently on other histories – from geology to Neolithic axe factories, mining and quarrying. He knew the life of the valley, its people and peregrines, the insects, ferns and rocks. This wide-ranging knowledge started from and always came back to the rocks, which were at the centre of everything. For this family of exceptional craftsmen, climbing was not a sport – it was fundamental to being in a place.

—

That year transformed my relationship with climbing. After six years of regular indoor climbing, interspersed with haphazard trips onto the rocks, this was the first time I had been properly cut off from the indoors scene. Forced to find another way to get my fix, as generations had done before me, I took to the rocks. The local stone provided the perfect entry point. In the Lakes, I got stuck into a great variety of climbs and crags; building up so much more of that experience which is integral to the craft of traditional climbing. And with increasing familiarity, I relaxed on those old volcanics and began to notice more. The colours and textures of the rock; the feel of the wind; sounds; plants; other creatures. I began to appreciate how rock climbing enables a distinctive understanding of landscape: an insight founded upon physical contact and bodily perception; an intimate, personal knowledge which can also extend outwards to encompass other aspects of the environment. In the Lakes, I began to develop an understanding of how the cultures of the people, plants, animals and rocks ran together, their lives and natures intermingling. And it was climbing, above all other activities, that helped me to realise this. Climbing helped me to feel at home in the Lakes, giving me a tool to access some of the depth, breadth and culture of that place.

Reaching this point of greater case on the rock was significant. It was no end point – it was a gateway. The horizon expanded and I met fresh challenges. My skirmish on the north face of Great Gable highlighted how many more elements come into play on a mountain crag. On those heights, weather, exposure, route-finding and the condition of the crag gave rise to an utterly distinctive scale and style of climbing. Those commanding routes in the high environment demanded something more. And whatever that was, it was something that I wanted to find. I wanted to climb in the lofty mountain spaces.

VI

CUILLIN II

GABBRO AND BASALT

Aparticular experience in a certain geographical location can bestow that place with the most powerful resonance. Imagine returning to your old school. As you meet all of those sights, sounds, smells and textures once again, a distinct set of feelings rush in. Emotions that you have not felt for an age come back sharply; the intervening time vanishes and you become that old person once again. This triggering – the result of the peculiar ways that memory, identity and place knit together – can construct the most striking psychological topology.

Four years after my epic on the Cuillin, I stood on the black and white sands of the beach at Glen Brittle and eyed the serrated mountain-line once again. While a crew of sandpipers, oystercatchers and redshanks picked over the shoreline, I looked up at the sunset-reddened ridge and visceral memories flooded in. Confusion, alarm, stress, exhaustion, disorientation, the sense of being completely and utterly overwhelmed.

Returning to the Cuillin, this time I had no illusions. I knew something of what that potent and imposing skyline meant. I knew what those rocks felt like – and how they made me feel. I was all too aware of the scale of the challenge; the physical and mental strain; the many ways that those rocks run rings around the unwary. They had made a deep impression. A sense of dread sat, unshakeable, in the pit of my stomach. I returned braced to relive that same awful emotional and physical experience. After that fateful twenty-six hours in my early twenties, the Cuillin had become a landscape of fear.

Nevertheless, despite my misgivings, once again I had my sights set upon that skyline. Last time, waking so late in Coire Lagan, it had not taken long for Andy and me to make a decision. My ankle was sore, and that was excuse enough for both of us. We packed up, turned our backs on the mountain and hobbled out down the glaciated slabs. But the Cuillin, with its convoluted line, crazy rock formations and heart-stopping drops, was such a compelling formation I couldn't let it rest. I wanted to link that line – to piece together the fragments – to grasp the Cuillin traverse in its entirety. I was not alone in my desire. This time I was with a crew of friends – nine experienced mountaineers and climbers – none of whom had set foot on the Cuillin before; all of whom aspired to complete the traverse.

We came up for a full week in late May; a week that just happened to be blessed with the most exceptional weather. Every day the sun shone, blazing bright through a clear blue sky. The bog shimmered, light rippling and bending in the heat rising from the crispy dry peat. Sunburn and heat rash prickled on our skin but the powerful rays did not sap our energy. High on sunshine, riding those enervating waves of light, day after day, we slogged up the punishing slopes to access the rocky crest overhead.

With a week of astonishing weather on our hands, we made the effort to familiarise ourselves with the Ridge. On the first day, we climbed the In Pinn via the South Crack and circled the great crest above Coire Lagan before plummeting like peregrines down the Great Stone Chute. On the second day, we scrambled up and down the five immense black pinnacles that lead onto the summit of Sgùrr nan Gillean – the most northerly peak on the Cuillin. On the third day, we packed our kit and, leaving Glen Brittle campsite mid-afternoon, began marching in across the bog. It was time.

The plan was clear. That afternoon and evening, we would climb Sgùrr nan Eag and Sgùrr Dubh Mòr before dropping down to bivi in Coir' a' Ghrunnda. From there, we would wake early, stash our sleeping kit behind some boulders and take on the rest of the traverse. If all went to plan, tomorrow evening we would finish up with a score of celebratory pints in the Sligachan.

———

A glorious evening: light stretched out, velvety shadows sinking blue behind the rocks and inside the corrie as the sun slipped down towards the western horizon. This would be a magical time to perch atop one of the sgùrrs or settle inside a corrie on the western flanks, drinking in the sunset and watching the Small Isles of Canna, Eigg and Rùm float like mystical apparitions levitating above a sea of light. But we were still crossing the brutal peridotite boulder field at the head of Garbh-choire. Four years on, and these cantankerous boulders were just as torturous as I remembered. Tired and hungry, I was ready to stop.

Instead, I trundled on, buoyed at this ebbing by the

company. I was with Stewart, Julie, Adam, Sandy, Bob, Anta, Tom and, just for good measure, a second Tom. We had taken the principle of 'the more the merrier' and set out as a party of nine. This was not exactly standard protocol. Unless you are as sure-footed as Finlay Wild, two is generally considered the best number for a Cuillin traverse since in a good partnership, you can move quickly, which – as I learned last time – is essential with so much technical ground to cover. A group of three has the advantage of lighter bags, better decision-making and more craic. (Morale is also vital.) After much deliberation and discussion, in which it was clear that everyone wanted to do the traverse, we had gone for an inclusive approach and set out as a full atypical nine. The fellowship of the Cuillin.

Scuttling back down through the frost-shattered scree and boulders, the bosom of Coir' a' Ghrunnda was moving into twilight as we finally made it to our resting ground. We ate late and stretched out in our bivi bags. Nine warm, breathing bodies lying like a covey of ptarmigans, nestled between the mountain rocks.

My sleep that night was utterly distinct from my last one on the Cuillin. Where Coire Lagan had held me comatose, collapsed, lost to the deepest, darkest, densest of sleeps, the small hours inside Coir' a' Ghrunnda passed in another state. It was one of those incredible northern midsummer evenings – an evening where night never really came. After the golden hour, one twilight followed another. Blue shadows settled into the sky and the stones, softening everything in a dusk that lingered, punctuated by a few stars and the looming silhouette of the corrie bowl, still present in the half-light. In this beguiling liminal space – the wonder of Scottish summer – I drifted in and out of sleep, relaxed and watchful, soothed and intrigued.

All that week my sleeps were strangely active. After each long day on the Ridge, I lay in my sleeping bag, glad to rest, but never slumping in a flummoxed state of fatigue. Something had switched. Instead, between passages of deep rest, my mind was busy. Through the long twilights, the Cuillin danced through my dreams in a spate of flickering images. Scree slopes. Pinnacles. A flake of rock, an incut step, a thin ledge around the precipice. A shattered orange basalt staircase. Each image pressed in: bold, vivid and important.

On my prior calamitous trip up to the Cuillin, as Andy and I trudged back out down the glaciated slabs, we met a mountain guide who was heading in with a couple of clients. We chatted, briefly, sharing our sorry story. He wanted details: where exactly was this loose rock? We explained. He listened closely, then nodded – ah yes – and headed on up the hill, leaving in his wake a sense of absolute astonishment. We had just met someone who knew the Cuillin in such detail that he could pinpoint the exact rock that I had pulled out. Such a depth of knowledge, encompassing so much complicated terrain, was completely incomprehensible to my tired, overwhelmed younger self. But on my return visit, as I slipped into those crazy dreamlands night after night, I came to understand how one might acquire that knowledge.

The rocks were incessant – running through my head all night – but they did not come as nightmarish ghouls. Rather, they were part of a scheme that my mind was working hard to fathom. As my body relaxed after each daily toil, my mind jumped in, playing catch up, seizing the chance to go over all the disjointed fragments, arranging them into scenes, trying to grasp the sequence. Repeating, revisiting, revising: I had never experienced such an active process of spatial memorisation before. Perhaps London taxi drivers go through something similar when they acquire the Knowledge. All that week my subconscious was consumed by a frenetic drive to commit the Cuillin constellation to heart.

—

Beep-beep-beep-beep: a chorus of Casio watch alarms broke the morning. Sighs. Yawns. A sliver of moon still sat in the inky sky. Rustling sleeping bags. Zips. The stomp of footfall as the quickest surfaced. The rocks around us were still dark but the sky was paling. An alpine start. Dutifully, I floundered fully dressed from my bivi bag as the first trio – Julie, Tom and Stewart – set off, haring up the northern slopes of Coir' a' Ghrunnda, making for the dim summit of Sgùrr Alasdair at the start of another long day on the Cuillin.

So high: so early. Like waking for an early morning flight, everything in those dawn hours had a touch of dreamy surrealism. With trudging up those rough slopes to Sgùrr Alasdair came a sense of waking with the slumbering rocks. The sky slowly lightened and the rocks gained detail and definition.

From the summit, fuzzy eyes looked down on thick banks of fleecy cloud, silently flowing over the sea and glens below, passing between openings in the mountains, delineating the sound. The eastern horizon was illuminated – the sun was creeping up – and the shadowed rocks began to blush pink as the first low rays hit the Cuillin. We had climbed into the sunrise. Held aloft in that golden-pink-blue dawn –

suspended in a realm of bewitching brilliance – we moved on, continuing along the awakening mountain.

Out of the scree, ramps and rough rocky lumps rose a mighty fin of rock. The Inaccessible Pinnacle stood sharp and clear in the morning light. The advance trio were already there, disappearing up into the great sky, now moving into a steady shade of daytime blue.

At the base rock, the other Tom, Bob and I clustered together, swiftly pulling rope, gear and harnesses out for our ascent. Later in the day this spot would be busy. Flocks of walkers and climbers would gather here, chattering and queuing. Some would stand stony-faced and world-weary; some wide-eyed with apprehension; others irritably jostling and muttering about 'punters'. But at this time, the rock was quiet.

When brothers Charles and Lawrence Pilkington first climbed this mighty obelisk in 1880, loose rock abounded. To free the line they had to prise out and hurl away a mountain of frost-shattered rubble, creating such a racket that 'the very rock of the pinnacle itself seemed to vibrate with indignation.'[19] On our day, Tom fluttered up the rocky rib with little sound aside from the occasional jangle of gear, the odd chuckle or exclamation and then, finally, the shout that bounded out over the abyss.

'Safe!'

The rope snaked up the fin and I waited, braced, a coiled spring, hands already on the cool rock, ready to start.

'On belay!'

'Climbing!'

I sprang on, hands clasping and releasing the rough blocks, reaching up for more as my feet nudged into the steps and ledges. Here was a flake: my hands gratefully wrapped around its defined toothy point. There was a crack: my fingers slotted in, embracing that secure sense of momentary enclosure.

The rib narrowed, heightening to an ever-sharpening point – with each movement higher, the exposure increased but, still flush with holds and grip, so even as the surface narrowed, the pinnacle felt dizzyingly accommodating, as though the rocks were pushing me up, raised higher and higher, towards some distant point, elevated above aeons of vertical space, teetering on the cusp of flight. Topping out in the sky, I joined Tom on the summit block where we shook our heads and beamed and sparkled, our eyes soaring over acres of air, the world laid out at our feet.

Abseiling down the back of the pinnacle, we caught up with Stewart, Julie and Tom, who sat waiting on the red roof of An Stac. Behind us came Sandy, Adam and Anta, dropping like spiders down their rope. At this point – now one third of the way along the Ridge – the trios disbanded. Merging back into a collective mass, we continued along the Ridge, heading into unknown territory in a fluid formation, variously fanning out and clustering back in together, according to the collective pace of nine moving bodies.

All along the crest, the features kept coming. There was Sgùrr na Banachdich, Sgùrr Thormaid and the Three Teeth. Then Sgùrr a' Ghreadaidh, the Wart, An Doras and Sgùrr a' Mhadaidh. Within this constant stream of peaks, pinnacles and troughs lay incessant technical challenges, each always demanding the utmost physical and mental attention. For so much of the Cuillin – with all of its heart-stopping exposure and savage drops – one wrong step, one slip, one loose rock would be fatal. Footwork, balance and hand–eye coordination were everything.

Yet this time, I did not cling tight in terror. Moving my body around the sharp, rocky forms was not a desperate strain; it was an intricate melody. I listened to the gabbro and the basalt, paying close attention, absorbing their intent while moulding my form around and within their contours. The architecture was so twisted, misshapen, improbable – and such fun to explore. White quartz veins ran across the bristling gabbro – in places standing out like razor-sharp spider webs; in other sections seeming more like bone marrow. Fine-grained basalt dykes and sills appeared like crazy paving, striking lines of shattered orange-blue steps or crude assemblages of musical keys from a long-defunct xylophone.

Padding across the sweeping slabs, edging around black pinnacles, bridging down steep corners, a magical flow developed. I loved hunting out the hidden holds and foot placements; uncovering all those amenable little features that appear like blessings in the harsh rocky desert of the Cuillin. Route-finding, I discovered, was an utterly absorbing and compelling process.

Gathering in beside Stewart, I listened closely as he stopped on some rocky knoll like a preacher on the mount, reading aloud directions from the guidebook.

'Don't go too high . . . Descend and keep to the left of the Wart . . . switch to the right-hand side with a couple of short down-climbs . . . The first top looks horrendous direct but can be passed by a path on the right . . .'

Armed with these brief instructions, Tom and I darted ahead to seek out our line through the morass. Stepping up ledges, peering around corners and lowering ourselves down walls, we forged on, calling across the rocks to one another, testing things out for the group. Up here? Will that go? Surely not that way . . .

'*Follow the crest to the first lump . . . Traverse on the right to reach a rock bridge . . . Take a short basalt chimney . . .*'

'Over here, Tom!'

'You found that basalt chimney?'

'Yep!'

'How is it?'

'Interesting!'

———

A raven perched on a pinnacle, its barks echoing across a dizzying cleft. I love hearing these feathered characters chatter across the corries and fly out from the rocks. Gliding, swooping, dropping, twirling, their winged play is mesmerising, revealing the currents surging and flowing all around this great rocky edge.

In preparing for the traverse, we had been warned about these clever corvids, who are the real masters of the Cuillin. They don't miss a trick. In other regions, ravens have a symbiotic relationship with wolves, alerting the pack to prey and following the canines to benefit from their kills. But with climbers and walkers in the Scottish mountains, ravens have a rather more one-sided relationship.

Quick to solve the riddle of an unattended rucksack, zips and lunchboxes present no barrier to these beguiling creatures and tales of their crafty pilfering abound across the mountain community. A particularly large king raven is said to preside over the towers of Buachaille Etive Mòr in Glencoe. On Ben Nevis, a recent climb put up by Iain Small and Dave MacLeod was named in honour of a certain wily black bird that heckled their ascent. While the climbers looked down from the route, a raven hopped over to their bags, unzipped two lid pockets, ate their sandwiches and threw the rest of the contents over the surrounding area. 'Luckily,' Iain explained, 'my car keys were clipped onto a tab.'[20] They named the climb Nevermore, after the Edgar Allan Poe poem, 'The Raven'.

—

Beyond the absorbing rocky immediacies, all that long day, the views from the Ridge were immense. Sunlight caught the water, setting Loch Coruisk sparkling, and twisting burns and lochans shone in the corries at our feet. On this beautiful blue midsummer day the Hebrides and the mainland mountains were constant companions – but as the day wore on, things flattened. We seemed to have been toiling over dry, grinding rocks in the blazing sunshine for aeons. Faces were red, feet hot and tired, water bottles nearly empty, eyes beginning to glaze into the thousand-mile stare.

Waiting for the tail end of our great party to catch up, I lay, face down in the gravel and thin grass, relieved to stretch out on the ground and close my eyes. Resting, for a moment, pressed into the darkness, was the most sublime spartan bliss. I had known the Cuillin would tire my legs and arms but I had never realised my eyes could feel so tired. The focus was relentless.

I was being consumed by the single-minded vision of the

climber. To pull off the piece – to perform the entire Cuillin traverse safely and successfully – I had to keep alert and focused; eyes on the ridge at all times. There was little space to see or comprehend anything beyond the most immediate matter.

That level of focus is exclusory; it is part of what can mark climbers out as blinkered monomaniacs. We can be so focused on the rock that we become partially deaf and blind to anything auxiliary. Other people, beings and wider contexts all fade into the background while the rock commands our fixated attention.

Yet there is also something transformative about maintaining eye contact with a geological feature. In giving your absolute attention to the mountain, you get to know aspects of that bigger, older living place in minute detail. Unlike the photographer who looks through a lens to freeze-frame the scene, capturing a single moment in time, the vision of the climber is always a three-dimensional unfolding. We study the matter at hand, feeling for insight, feeding that knowledge into the bodymind, which is actively negotiating the world at our fingertips. We look in order to move with the mountain.

—

The final push. Am Basteir, the penultimate peak, reared up, sharp, loose and alive. Like a dragon, this towering blade of rock awaits, poised; a savage sting in the tale. With our large cast of adventurers, we had already made the decision not to take on the challenge of the Basteir Tooth. The classic line tackles this formidable feature via an airy traverse and the sharp technicalities of Naismith's Route. But moving as a nine, there was no time for us all to rope up and climb. Instead, the amoeba dropped down, skirting through a late-lying snowfield tucked into the base of Am Basteir, before turning back on ourselves and pulling steeply back up onto the summit of the Executioner. As with most things on the Cuillin, the 'easy' line brought its own challenge.

Running down from the jagged crest of the Cuillin come cascades of loose rock, swelling out into great rivers of scree composed of all the fragments that have fallen away from those great rugged walls and tops, all streaming away down the mountain sides. The word scree comes from the old Norse *skriða,* meaning landslide, and indeed, to set foot on scree is to feel the earth move beneath your feet, constantly; to sense the active process by which the Cuillin is shifting and redefining, constantly, with each loose piece marking another part of the Ridge that has chipped away, fallen out, leaving behind a sharper, leaner form. Of the many scree slopes that litter the Cuillin, the most significant pour down into Coire Lagan, where the Great Stone Chute and An Stac screes hold billions of loose stones that fan out into vast rocky aprons.

Stomp slide; stomp slide; stomp slide: ascending scree is soul-crushing drudgery. With each step, I looked carefully, selecting the most promising footing within a mass of inse-cure fragments. I placed the boot with optimism – perhaps this one won't slide – but with each weighting comes a critical point where, with a heart-sinking grind, the frag-ments collapse and the foot slips down. Head down: keep going. There is no real art to climbing a scree slope. It is, quite literally, an exercise in dragging your feet. All the way up the steep sliding fin of Am Basteir, we sweated, grunted, swore and muttered, everybody straining hard, everyone caught up in their own private battle of wills.

———

Sgùrr nan Gillean: the Peak of Young Men. Like Sgùrr Alasdair for Alexander Nicolson, Sgùrr Mhic Chòinnich for John Mackenzie, Sgùrr Thormaid for Norman Collie and Sgùrr Thearlaich for Charles Pilkington, here was one more top on that ridgeline named for men. But this one had a particular significance setting it apart from all the others.

One by one, our bodies piled up onto that last top, some pausing to wearily punch the air before collapsing to join the clan lying packed like sardines on this small patch of hallowed high ground.

'Flippin' epic.'

We had made it.

A panorama of drained wonder. Sea lochs and islands and peninsulas circled around us, all hazy and soft in the late-afternoon sunshine. A pod of white clouds drifted like whales through the gleaming archipelago of Sleat, Soay, Minginish, Duirinish, Waternish, Trotternish, the Uists, Harris, Lewis and Raasay. Raasay, where the poet Sorley MacLean had grown up, looking across to the Cuillin every day, seeing the mountain in all its seasons, weathers and moods. With that prospect in mind, he dreamed of liberty for all mankind, which is realised through his image of *a' Chuilithinn 's e 'g èirigh*. The Cuillin that is rising.

Lying there, leaning into the exhaustion, draining the final drops of water from long-empty bottles, beaming smiles broke out across hot, tired faces. We high-fived and back-slapped and joked in weary delirium while the Ridge stretched out, fading and shimmering in the heat, a serrated line of improbable dimensions. Had we really been on top of the Inaccessible Pinnacle earlier that day? It looked so far, so distant, a dream vision – a mere small pimple on the mighty dragon's back of relentlessly ruptured rough ground.

Last time, my encounter with the Cuillin had been so fraught I nearly came completely undone. But today, returning with this big crew, I had reached a point where I could meet and hold the Cuillin's gaze. On this long midsummer day we had met the rocks of the Cuillin. Together, we had grasped the rising ground and ascended with it.

Yet there was still another step to go. Having made the final top, all eyes dropped down to a small white building that beckoned from across the bog. The Sligachan. The carrot at the end of the stick. If we moved now, we would make it down well before last orders and so, in a daze of rocky exhaustion, we dragged our bones off the summit and carried on, back past the rocky window, tumbling out of the mountain down through Coire a' Bhasteir.

The screes in descent provided the most miraculous drop – hundreds of metres lost in mere minutes – a laborious process of thigh-burning knee-shattering one-at-a-time steps completely bypassed. The art of descending scree is to pay attention and relax. Loosen up. Accept that the rocks will send your legs flying. Instead of holding back, let go. Shift your mind into the soles of your feet to follow the utterly unpredictable movements of the rocks. This way, speed, gravity and momentum become your friends, allowing you to pour down the mountain with fluid, grinding ease, tumbling, like a rolling stone, back down into the world of earth, plant and water.

Finally tramping out across the long easy flat bogland, a beautiful state of tired elation began to set in. I smiled, remembering my trepidation some hours – or days, or was it years ago? – when I had returned to the Cuillin braced to relive the same dreadful experience of my early twenties. I had expected to feel drained and overwhelmed; for the rocks to run rings around me; to reach some kind of breaking point somewhere along the skyline. But that had not happened. Stopping beside a burn, I plunged my sore fingers into the sun-warmed waters, splashing handfuls of the lovely liquid across my face, before filling my bottle and pouring the crystal-clear waters down my parched throat. With the slightly delirious post-climb exhaustion came a sense of having completed something much bigger than the Cuillin. I had tested my body – I had pushed it harder than I had ever done before – and, defying all my expectations, it had performed the piece, no problem. An elated inner voice told me that my mountain apprenticeship had been served.

In the days that followed, we packed up and left, rolling back down traffic-laden roads and motorways on our long journey south. While our tired bodies gradually relaxed and recovered on that happy sunny journey, the glow continued. We chatted over the highs and lows, laughing and reliving the many moments we had all been through on those long mountain days. We had our photos and our stories and also somewhere inside that euphoria lay a treasured sense of those commanding Cuillin rocks, now traversed, somehow being part of us, written into our muscles and memories, forging a new vein of possibility within the psyche.

VII

DINORWIG

SLATE/LLECHI

PERGYL! Hen chwarel
DANGER! Old quarry workings
Dim mynediad
Do not enter

Leaving Dinorwig village tramway behind, clambering over fences, ignoring signs and padlocks, pacing up shattered slate staircases, passing roofless huts, we trudge up towards the big pit, bags loaded with climbing gear. Finally, we walk through the stone archway that leads into our destination, completely unprepared for the sight that greets us. From this entrance platform, we survey the crater in utter astonishment. Terrace after terrace circles around the rim, plummeting down into a terrible rocky opening.

A sheep bleats and the sound echoes across the titanic pit strewn with so much rubble and debris and shattered rock. Blocks the size of cars, buses or houses litter the hillside, all perched precariously atop one another. Old rusting pipes, cogs, wheels, tramlines and ladders protrude here and there, standing out sharp orange within the mass of dark, jagged broken matter. It all looks so precarious; so hard to get a sense of scale. Eyes adjust and start to pick out forms within the chaos. A black rectangle – a doorway – far across the pit on the opposite level; a series of decrepit slate huts and buildings lined-up, looking ridiculously tiny. From somewhere below my feet, down in the damp mossy depths, comes the sound of dripping water.

Among all the spoil, rubble and rusting industrial debris, great slate slabs circle and plunge down into the deepening core of the mountain. In stark contrast to the chaos of choss, the geometries of these faces are startling. All the blasting and extraction work has created a magnificent body of cliffs – divided and split; severed and cracked – a feast of shadowed overhangs and sheer shining faces.

Some are black as coal, where water seeps, flows and drips down the exposed rock. Other aspects radiate light, shining lilac-grey with the luminous quality of a watercolour. Rippling lines dance across certain surfaces – streaks of white and turquoise that stand out against the darker purple rock face like the aurora borealis in the night sky. The mind somersaults as it realises that these distinctive lines mark bands of matter that dropped to a seabed some 500 million years ago.

Dinorwig is a striking presence within this corner of Snowdonia. Across the valley, in the village of Llanberis, where the steam train carries visitors up to the summit of Snowdon and hordes of outdoors enthusiasts congregate in pubs, shops and the fabled Pete's Eats café, the mountains of slate waste are all too visible. The spoil tips sit below Elidir Fawr, a mighty peak shaped like a boar's back, whose name is tied to an ancient Celtic warrior-prince, but is now better known as Electric Mountain, after the power station that hums with hydroelectric energy generated deep inside the quarried mountain. When the sky is heavy, as it so often is in north Wales, all those millions of tonnes of exposed waste slate darken, taking on a sinister, imposing character.

——

My hands slide across the surface until my fingers find something positive. There: an edge. Fingers grip tight, locking onto the cold slate. Toes follow fingers, stepping onto tiny edges. Calf, thigh and stomach muscles contract, pulling my body into the rock and up to a new ledge where my eyes and fingers hungrily hunt for the next step.

This is new territory. I have never climbed on slate before and so I move with focused attention, letting my senses investigate. Like a cautious swimmer, I wade in slowly, letting my body adjust to the temperature, watching closely for currents and jellyfish. I don't want to get stung.

Tapping suspect blocks, I listen closely for the telltale sound of hollow rock. I pull cautiously on the razor-sharp slate slivers. It all seems so delicate; so friable. Could they snap? What if I place a foot on a slab? Will it slide off?

The slabs have an uneven finish and opportunities lie in the rough edges. I cling to fractures, lumps, cracks and protrusions. Halfway up, I meet a distinctive runnel, an inch wide and a metre long. I squeeze three fingers into the bottom of the old drill line and step up, moving with delicate precision.

While the vast quarry space is alienating, up close, there is something strangely familiar about this rock. Pulling myself into the smooth purple-green surface, I meet an unexpected surge of homely feeling. Throughout my life, this rock has been part of my homescape. All the rented terraces, flats, cottages and tenements of my twenties – buildings in Liverpool, Leeds, Grasmere and Scotland, almost every house I have lived in across the UK – has been roofed by slate. Before that, I grew up in a house where my father had hammered the slates onto the roof himself. A full-time builder, he used his evenings and weekends to build a home for his family. (His favourite slates are Caernarfon Reds.)

As I negotiate the steep angles, smooth surfaces and sharp edges of the slate slabs, I wonder whether this would feel familiar to him. While he has spent his working life in awkward settings that demand physical strength and agility (clambering up and down ladders, crawling through loft spaces and labouring on exposed roof pitches), he has never rock-climbed – none of my family have. They love walking but, for them, climbing is an alien activity. The risks seem monumental, the rewards unfathomable. Until I wrote this book, I rarely spoke to them about climbing. I felt certain that, no matter what I said, they just wouldn't get it and I couldn't face the fear-fuelled disapproval. However, like a painter has to paint or a dancer must dance, I have to climb.

It was this growing sense of climbing as an artistic practice – a way of looking, questioning and opening up the world – that brought me to this industrial landscape. I came to Dinorwig when my outdoor climbing craft had developed to a point where I could see past the thrills and fear and had reached a new understanding of the process. Unlike walking, where I could happily trundle absent-mindedly through a place, letting my focus and thoughts wander from this thing to that, in climbing, attentive observation is not a choice. It is essential.

On the rock, eyes scrutinise tiny details alongside bigger features, sequences and vast environments; bringing all of the parts together in an effort to comprehend that place at that moment. But the eye cannot tell me enough. Skin – the largest organ in the human body – is also crucial to the process of sensory information gathering. Touch reveals things that the eye could never grasp. Many aspects of the outer environment are thus deliberately brought inside; internalised within the climbers' being – where they are put to immediate use. Every detail, every piece of information that my senses glean, is intuitively processed and put to work by the whole body, which is engaged in the immersive multi-dimensional physical task of climbing. Working closely with geology – reaching in, pulling out and performing the shapes that lie within the rocks – is a collaborative movement in which the climber embodies the landscape.

———

Our next route follows a distinctive groove that arcs up and right. But the edges feel wrong. The angles are off. My hands struggle for comfortable positions and my feet must be placed as carefully as a ballerina en pointe – only I'm wearing the wrong shoes. Unlike gritstone – where you slap your foot onto a blank wall aiming to conjure a forceful friction between rubber and rock – slate has no friction. This rock requires absolute precision. Miss the spot and your foot shoots off. I'm wearing my dependable trad slippers, which are perfect for long mountain routes, but on these short, sharp quarried edges, I would be better in a pair of tight performance shoes with arched soles, concentrating weight and power into the toes. Such unforgiving rock demands discomfort.

Pushing on up the wall, my hands and feet dance around the peculiar edges. Towards the top, the groove gives way to a slab. The holds become sparser and ever more precise. I reach a thin turquoise shelf and find a dark line of water running along it. By now, I've learned enough about slate to know that if I step in the water, my foot will slide straight off – a wild release that could throw everything off balance.

I hunt around. There is nowhere else. My foot has to go onto this little shelf. I look closer. There is a tiny dry spot – the size of a penny. I place my toe on carefully and press down, stepping up. A rush of heat floods my body – but my foot stays on. The tension holds and I reach up for the chains.

'Okay, Adam,' I shout down. He takes in the slack: I weight the rope and he lowers me off the wall, back down to join him and Anna on the level.

In our little team of three, we work a small bay of rock – a cluster of quarried blocks, slabs and undercuts – looking out the lines that will open the rock and open our bodies. We take it in turns: one person climbs, another belays and the third watches on, calling up advice and encouragement. When the climber descends back down to the level, we shift roles.

Not so long ago, a different group occupied this space. A crew of four Welsh quarrymen dressed in corduroy trousers, hobnailed boots and flat caps. (The earlier nineteenth-century quarrymen had equally distinctive style: they wore white fustian jackets, flannel shirts, flannel trousers and a bowler hat.) This slate bay would have been their bargain – their working rock face – that they had negotiated from the steward. To strike the bargain, the men were able to read the rock extremely closely. A good bargain was highly sought after: there the slate peeled away in delicious slabs, *fel menyn*, like butter. The bad bargains were full of convoluted rock that was beset with defects: curls, veins, joints, faults and dense, hard rock.

No helmets, no harnesses: to release the slate from the mountain, the quarrymen hung from ropes tied around waists and looped around thighs while they levered, wrenched, hammered, drilled and blasted away the very rocks that they stood upon. Their physical knowledge of the slate must have been extraordinary. Glimpses of that expertise can be found in the language. In the mines of Blaenau Ffestiniog, a vein of slate was known as a *llygad*, an eye: when the quarrymen opened the rock, they saw it as opening up the slate's eye. Among the veins in that huge seam of slate, there was Llygad Bach (Little Eye), Llygad Coch (Red Eye), Llygad Newydd (New Eye) and Hen Llygad (Old Eye). The division of labour within the quarries followed the language. Those who worked the rock face spoke Welsh; the capitalists who owned the site and sold the finished slates spoke English. It was therefore proudly asserted that slate spoke Welsh.

Unfortunately, none of our crew speaks fluent slate.

As Anna climbs, I look out again, trying once more to grasp the scale of this place. We're climbing in a pit called Australia, the largest quarried area in Dinorwig. In this vast stony amphitheatre, sounds bounce off the walls and galleries, echoing through the empty air. Atop one of the nearby skylines, a climber leans over the edge, shouting commands to his partner.

'Take it steady STEADY
When you're ready READY.'

Water drips. Occasional feet set the loose slate clattering. A high-pitched mewl calls out from one of the distant corners. Child? Goat? Peregrine? In this eerie opening it is hard to place anything with absolute certainty.

Once, this quiet scene must have roared with life and noise and activity. Hammering, drilling, blasting. Shouts, rockfall, explosives. The smell of iron, sweat and sulphur; clouds of thick white dust. Men hanging off ropes, everywhere. The screech of cogs, wheels and machinery; wagons rolling along the levels and down the inclines, conveying the slate out of the mountain down to the workshops, where the stones met the blow of hammer and chisel; split and ordered, neat stacks of oblong roofing slates were loaded up in hundreds of tonnes, every day, onto another fleet of wagons that were driven, steaming and chugging along tramlines, down to the port where these pieces of Elidir Fawr were shipped out around the British Empire.

—

The wind picks up. Bitter gusts blast into the open pit, shaking the stumps of brittle brown heather. Mist drifts over the hilltop and drizzle comes and goes – light specks fall, producing dark blemishes on the teal slate. Moments later, the marks vanish. It is October and under such leaden skies, even the grass seems grey.

The damp chill starts to penetrate. I pile on a woolly

hat, another jumper, a coat, but even with these extra layers my fingers and toes still continue to numb and muscles clench tight. The slate grows colder. In blazing summer sunshine, slate could cook eggs; today it handles like a mortuary slab.

After a few more routes and some cold sandwiches, we cut our losses and call it a day. Packing away the rope, we leave Australia, walking back out of that immense pit via the broken rattling slopes we came in on. But instead of retreating to a warm haven – and at this moment, the bright, light, cosy world of Pete's Eats in Llanberis is exercising the most powerful pull – we stay in Dinorwig. We are curious about another climbers' route in the quarry. This one is longer and more exploratory; a wandering line that weaves around the vast workings, making use of the network of old tunnels, ladders, holes, levels and passageways created by the quarrymen moving around their workplace.

Scuttling around like three goats, we pick our way over loose gravelly slopes that slide down towards the emerald depths of a quarry pool below. We are not interested in the surface matter of Dali's Hole – the walls, waters and occasional trees do not hold our attention – we are looking for a black hole; a hidden hole; the tunnel entrance that marks the start of Snakes and Ladders.

We find the hole and head into the darkness.

Light. Water. Greenery. The tunnel leads out to a vertical chasm where the sky is distant, framed overhead by a great wedge-shaped cutting. A waterfall pours down the rock face and ferns and mosses grow in thick clusters on all of the enclosed, wet, dripping surfaces.

Meeting this unexpected scene, my sense of the present

collapses. Despite the decaying brickwork, I feel as though we have passed through aeons of geological time and emerged somewhere in the deep past.

Perhaps the Triassic time of dinosaurs, some 240 million years ago. Or maybe earlier still – the first ferns appear in fossils from 360 million years ago. Moss is older again. Ancestors of the lush green pillows before me spread across the planet 470 million years ago; absorbing carbon dioxide and dissolving rocks, these powerful plants transformed the planet and triggered an Ordovician ice age. Back then, all of the rock upon which I stand was sat deep underwater in layers of sedimentary stone yet to be uplifted, folded and metamorphosed into slate.

Dinorwig does the strangest things with time.

Tripping over rusted old railway lines, we continue through the next tunnel and come out in another vast quarry hole. Here the ground is strewn with shattered slate blocks and fragments, forming a treacherous sea of fangs and daggers that we must pick our way across, making for a set of iron chains.

At the top of the chains, another dark tunnel leads us on through the mountainside and then back out into the light, where we scuttle through yet more sliding slate chippings, hunting for another black hole. This one is completely improbable. We walk towards a sheer wall of slate. At the bottom, there is a pile of rocks and between the rocks – a tiny black hole. Peering into the darkness, I make out a few stones. Some gravel. Beyond that, everything is black.

It's a tight squeeze so I take off my rucksack and slide down the rock, belly on boulder, back against the wall, legs reaching through darkness until my feet hit on something that feels like solid ground. I slither down and the ground, unexpectedly, holds.

Once inside, my eyes slowly adjust. The walls are rough and the roof high. For some reason, this tunnel has been blocked off. Rockfall, perhaps.

Looking down, far away through the blackness, there is a small circle of light.

Anna and Adam drop down, joining me in the darkness, and we walk along the tunnel, following the old train tracks, careful to avoid stepping in the pools of water. The further we go, the more the darkness deepens, pressing in, black and awful. Depth is thrown. Distance becomes illusive. We pace through a black eternity. But gradually, as our legs keep moving, the circle of light swells.

Finally, we emerge blinking onto a gleaming slope of shattered rocks. Scree, sky, cliffs, moss, terraces, rusty pipes: it takes a moment to make sense of it all. We have come out in Australia. The geography of this place is mind-boggling. Sometimes a climb helps to make sense of challenging geographies. The process of working closely with the rock and following a line through vast, complex terrain can simplify matters, bringing a sense of order; but the order of Dinorwig is no easy thing to grasp. It doesn't help that the entire place is moving. Loose stones clatter, shift and slide beneath our feet. The walls above are clearly constantly changing, fracturing and falling. This place is restless. Unstable.

———

From this low point towards the base of Australia, we make a rising traverse, scuttling around broken, insecure ledges where blocks tumble away, rattling and crashing down into the depths below. I am reminded of the Cuillin and all those airy precarious lines that must be approached with utmost attention and care – care for myself, but also care for my comrades. In these sketchy places we move together, with a mind for one another. Dangerous environments demand strong teamwork and a deep understanding between partners.

That's one of the things that I love about climbing. In the unforgiving vertical regions, there is no room for bluff, bluster or pretence. On the rock face, the veneer is stripped away and you can see the heart and mettle of a person. This insight is one of the many privileges of a climbing relationship, and it can help to build the most profound bonds between very different people. The presence of danger, which we are always trying to mitigate, brings us closer together.

For the quarrymen who created this perilous landscape, the camaraderie must have run far deeper. Constantly orchestrating rockfall, dislodging immense blocks of crushing weight and razor-sharp slate edges, the communication and collaboration between the quarrymen must have been next level. During the peak of the industry, a vast team of 3,500 men worked in Dinorwig; when the quarry closed in 1969, that number had reduced to 350. Despite the danger and hardships, when the Dinorwig quarry closed, many men missed it. They missed the crew, the camaraderie and the work that had shaped their life since they were boys.

But as well as the lighter side of Dinorwig, there was also a terrible darkness. The human cost of such intensive physical work was immense. Accidents happened often. Fingers lost. Legs crushed. Limbs amputated in the on-site hospital.

When someone died at work, the whole site knew, more or less straightaway, and the quarrymen laid down their tools and went home for the rest of the day. At the widow's house, a special clean white cloth was laid out on a table by the front door and a big dish was placed in the centre for collection towards the funeral cost. Everyone contributed. Between 1822 and 1969, 362 men died in Dinorwig.

The suffering went beyond the accidents. Physical toil, working in extreme environments, poor diet and poor living conditions all took their toll. Dust was pernicious. Whether drilling, blasting, chiselling or splitting, any action that breaks slate apart releases tiny particles that are easily inhaled, which then linger, like asbestos, in the lungs, damaging the soft tissue. Silicosis was common in the quarrymen, causing coughs, shortness of breath, chest infections, heart disease and lung cancer. In Blaenau Ffestiniog, the life expectancy of a quarryman was just thirty-eight. In these green valleys, so many lives were cut tragically short.

Immense fortunes were made from the slate quarries but, as is the way, the wealth was not evenly distributed. Wages were poor. In 1900, in an effort to improve working conditions, all 2,800 men walked out of Penrhyn Quarry, Bethesda. The Great Strike of Penrhyn was the longest dispute in British industrial history. The strike lasted for three years, creating three years of brutal privation in Bethesda. Homes were cold and dark. Schools closed. Some men left to seek work elsewhere. Some women turned to prostitution. Those who broke the strike were branded *bradwr* (traitor). But Lord Penrhyn did not yield. While families struggled to survive, the quarry owner was comfortably ensconced in Penrhyn Castle, an opulent mansion built from the profits of slate, sugar and slavery. To this day, the bitter impact of the strike is still felt within the community. Families were divided and the wounds may never fully heal.

In *Un Nos Ola Leuad* (*One Moonlit Night*), Caradog Prichard captures a year of poverty, loss, grief and madness in a quarrying village. His lyrical novel is loosely based on his own childhood in Bethesda. When Prichard was a baby his father died in a quarrying accident, so his mother brought the boys up alone, in poverty and with worsening mental health, until she was admitted to a mental hospital, where she lived out the rest of her days.

Kate Roberts, a towering figure within the twentieth-century Welsh language, literature and nationalism movements, portrayed the constant struggle that a typical quarrying family faced trying to get by on the pittance that the men earned in the quarries. *Traed mewn Cyffion* (*Feet in Chains*) details the day-to-day hardships by following the life of Jane Grufydd, who marries a quarryman and brings up their family of six children. The novel is based on personal experience. Roberts grew up in a quarrying village in north Wales and her father was a quarryman; she wrote *Feet in Chains* when she was living in the valleys of south Wales, another industrialised region where the coal-mining communities suffered epic hardships.

Both of these books contain heart-rending stories. Both made me cry. Through the immersive, charming and deeply disturbing pages of *One Moonlit Night*, I plunged into a child's experience of life around the quarries. In that confusing world, the child-narrator is surrounded by troubled people and troubling incidents. Friends, neighbours and family members disappear: some leave; some die. The child must cope with loss after loss after loss. *Feet in Chains* places that cruelty within a bigger frame. Reading about the hopes, pains, fears, thoughts and losses of one quarrying wife and mother, I burned with rage and anguish. Roberts humanises the quarries while exposing the brutal inhumanity of the wider system. Her book reveals the true cost of slate. Structural injustices are written into the billions of slates sitting on roofs across the world.

—

To leave Australia, we clamber up a series of iron ladders, forged by fires in the foundry at the foot of the quarry. These long lines, variously bolted, chained or roped to the rock, are now cold and rusty. They link the levels; although often, one ladder is not enough for these huge faces and so, upon reaching the top of one line, in mid-air we must step across a gaping void to clamber onto the foot of the next ladder. Such aerodynamic moves set the arches of my feet tingling. We climb slowly, gasping at the exposure, moving cautiously where the decrepit ladders are missing rungs and wobble with our weight. Yet at one time, the quarrymen will have run up and down these lines with fluid, unthinking ease.

Clinging to the rungs, my mind is with the quarrymen. Where my hands are now – fingers wrapped tight around the sturdy, cold iron – theirs must also have been, countless times before. I think of the calloused textures of those hands – transformed by so much exposure to rock, tools, ropes, chains and weather. When I was little I sometimes shrank away from my dad's worn builder hands. His skin could be horribly rough, especially in winter, when the work kept him out in the cold and wet. Then, his warm palms split apart, opening into seams and cracks that bled and wept.

Such hard-worn hands remained remarkably deft. Not only did the quarrymen drill, chisel, split, chip, trim, blast and hammer the slate for a living; but in their free time they also crafted beautiful pieces of stone artwork. A friend sent me a photo of a collection of slate whistles made by her great-grandfather, Lewis Henry Jones, who worked on the rock in Dinorwig, suspended on a rope, tapping to make space for explosives. The whistles, carefully displayed on a piece of white fabric, look like artefacts from a museum collection. But the whistles are not on public display. They are part of family lore, kept in the home and passed down through the generations.

There are four whistles – two black, two olive-green – and each is a tiny piece of geometric wonder. The finish is so fine, the details so sharp, the lines so precise that they look as though they were carved from wood or ivory. But this is slate, and these little stone whistles are a testament to the skill with which the Welsh quarrymen handled their rock; breathing life into cold, sharp matter.

——

Pulling up over the top of one last rusty ladder, we make it out of Australia and trundle into the sky on a wide grassy platform. We are at the apex of the quarry, high above the mounds of loose lilac chippings and deep plummeting holes, up at the point where the industry gives way to the mountain. Views stretch back down to Llanberis village and out to the coastal lowlands, the Menai Strait and Anglesey. Yet once again, this new vista does not help to put things in perspective. The quarry does not shrink to a comprehensible size – the scale expands. From here, I look down to the old ports where the slate was loaded and shipped out around the world. And over on Anglesey, although I cannot make them out, there are yet more homes where quarrymen rose at three every Monday morning to walk to the ferry, leaving their family for the week to work and sleep in the roughest barracks in Dinorwig.

A cluster of old buildings stand on this lofty platform. They are remarkably intact. We make for a long one that has solid walls, a reasonably sound-looking roof and glass windows. We circle around and find the door. It is hanging slightly off its hinges and a small metal notice has been nailed to the wooden panels: 'No Door to Door Salespeople'. Adam, playing the role of gentleman, lifts the door, holding it open for us to traipse inside.

A rusted old stove stands in the middle of a large, open room. Above the greening floor, the walls are whitewashed, although the rendering is crumbling and falling away in places, exposing the slate blockwork. Scratched graffiti cuts through the plaster. *DYLEN. LESLEY + KEN 1992. PNUT BUTTA CREW 2013.* Tattered jackets hang from pegs and beside a rusting kettle a row of crumbling leather work boots are lined up against the wall. This is an old *caban*, the bait room, where the quarrymen gathered at lunchtime.

Today the caban feels quiet, damp and decrepit; but this was once the heart and soul of the quarries. Picture a kettle steaming and stewing on the stove at the centre of the room. The quarrymen were furious tea drinkers and they had their own most particular way of preparing the brew. Their tea was not of the genteel tradition, where the water is lightly coloured by a passing touch of fragrant leaf. Half an hour before the lunch whistle went, a boy was sent to fill the caban kettle with water, tea and sugar. This infusion then sat stewing on the stove for a full thirty minutes before the men poured in, rattling their enamel mugs, ready for a cup of knock-your-socks-off quarryman's tea. They really knew how to get the most out of those precious leaves. (The quarry doctors tried to discourage this style of tea brewing since such long stewing caused health problems. The extreme tannin could produce liver cancer and other issues.)

Thus warmed and restored, the men were ready for something different. Each caban was governed by a president and committee who organised lunchtime activities. To complement all their physical labour, lectures and discussions were held on topics ranging from politics to current affairs, chapel, charity work and union matters. The quarrymen of north Wales took education seriously. Bangor University was built with donations from quarrymen who wanted to provide an education for their children. But they also enjoyed themselves. Eisteddfodau – competitive performances of music, poetry and literature – were popular inside these cultured hearts. Once upon a time, this tatty old building at the top of the quarry was filled with Welsh voices, laughter and song.

Like the quarryman's tea, Welsh song is a magical stimulant. There is nothing else like it. Growing up on the mid-Wales border, my education was steeped in Welsh language and culture, and we always sang together in school assemblies. There were the fun songs like 'Cyfri'r Geifr' ('Counting the Goats'), a Welsh tongue-twister which gathers pace as the goats we count take on more and more ridiculous colours, the whole song accelerating into a dizzying cacophony of mangled vowels and plosives. We also sang songs of great energy and emotion, like 'Hen Wlad Fy Nhadau', 'Land of my Fathers', in which our little lungs always belted out the rousing chorus: '*Gwlad! GWLAD! pleidiol wyf i'm gwlad.*' ('Country! Country! I am faithful to my country.') My favourite though, with its sincere, sweet and heartfelt lyricism, is 'Calon Lân'.

> *Nid wy'n gofyn bywyd moethus,*
> *Aur y byd na'i berlau mân:*
> *Gofyn wyf am galon hapus,*
> *Calon onest, calon lân.*

> *Not a life I ask of plenty*
> *Gold and gems are not for me:*
> *I desire a happy heart,*
> *an honest heart, a pure heart.*

There is something about this particular song that chokes me up. I cannot just listen to it – if I do not sing, the emotion forces its way out in tears – better to open the chest, let the words out and sing. I am not alone in my affection for this old hymn: 'Calon Lân' is now a rugby anthem, sung by tens of thousands of proud Welsh men and women in stadiums across Europe. With my back to the caban, looking out from the grassy platform at the top of Dinorwig, goosebumps prickle at the idea of a Welsh choir standing out here, shoulder to shoulder, singing together in a magical outpouring expression of valley, quarry, mountain, sea and air.

Outdoor art has a unique power. It is part novelty – art is so often housed within the built environment. Think culture: think city. There our galleries, museums, cinemas and theatres bring artworks and performances to large audiences. But while the walls and ceilings protect the pieces, they also shut them off from the wider natural environment. When art is performed in the outdoors – whether music, dance, theatre or story – there is always an air of spontaneity. Things creep in, unplanned and uninvited. A pair of ravens fly chattering overhead and the audience looks up, open and curious. A sunny day full of skylarks brings a blessed air. Rain comes in, dampening the spirits, making participation a waterproofed ordeal, but from that shared suffering comes a greater sense of unity. We have been through something, together. The simple act of gathering, with others, in the outdoors adds a layer of importance and the site inevitably draws geography into the piece, altering the audience's perception of that place and its environment. The work might force people to look a little closer; it might give them a new angle, a new understanding, a new point of connection. Art can be unsettling. It makes us think and feel.

The songs and stories of Welsh folk culture, passed down through the generations, are rooted in the landscape. They tell how this place came to be, charting folk heroes and villains as well as writing giants, dragons and magicians into the rocks and hills. Such stories contain echoes of truths now lost. The Welsh storying of landscape inspired Tolkien's epic fantasy, *The Lord of the Rings*. Sindarin, the Elven language he created, was informed by Welsh, and he was well versed in *The Mabinogion*, a medieval collection of myths and legends, charting great heroes, adventures, battles and magical misdeeds that took place across the hills, valleys and plains of Wales.

We practise this culture, keeping it alive, by sharing the stories and repeating the songs. Stories that I heard as a girl (sat cross-legged on the carpet tiles of my school assembly hall) I now repeat out on the hill. On glimpsing the snowy flanks of Cadar Idris from the top of another hill, I reach into my memory and share the story of the giant Idris with my English friend. Idris, one of the great astronomers, used to sit on top of that mountain and gaze at the stars, philosophising on the meaning of life and the fate of mankind. Such storying brings character and personality to these distinctive topographies, giving us more to say about the place, beyond simply naming. Creative geography feeds the imagination, and the social nature of these sharings enriches human relationships with natural places.

New artworks can achieve something different. Over a year-long residency at Penrhyn Castle in 2017, artists Zoe Walker and Neil Bromwich produced a performance piece called *Llechi a Llafur / Slate or State*. The artwork tackled a big and fraught subject: the history of the castle and its relationship with the community of Bethesda. Inside the castle (now owned by the National Trust), there was little acknowledgment of its connection to the quarry beyond an oil painting from 1832 by Henry Hawkins, which depicts the slate quarry in a Tower of Babel scene of heaving industry. Outside the castle, the legacy of the Great Strike was still deeply felt by the community. The hardship, betrayals and gross inequality had not been forgotten. Many took a strong stance and declared they would never set foot inside the castle.

Working with the people of Bethesda, Walker and Bromwich created an artwork that finally brought the community's voices and the missing history of the strike into Penrhyn Castle. The artists constructed a sculpture of the quarry that was shouldered and carried, like an oversized coffin, by the people in a grand procession from Bethesda to the castle. Men and women – descendants of strikers and quarrymen – walked in and sang, filling the echoing, opulent chambers with their Welsh voices. This piece helped the community to move into a new place – a difficult place – but one which they could occupy, finally, with a greater sense of agency, in a new reckoning with their heavy history.

—

Leaving the lofty caban behind, we follow a path that trails on in the direction of Snowdon, the mighty mountain known in Welsh as Yr Wyddfa, the Burial Place. Today the massif is hidden inside a heavy weight of grey cloud. We find another loose path and drop down into a little valley that leads to a cutting between two towering slate walls. Through the blasted cleft, a new space opens out. At our feet, the ground drops away, sharp. We are on the precipice of yet another pit. To access this one, we must abseil.

Fortunately, someone has drilled shiny silver anchor chains into the rock and we thread our rope through the metal ring, coiling up the ends before tossing them out, wheeling through space, gravity tugging the ends down to the ledge below. One at a time, we feed the rope through our belay devices and begin walking backwards over the edge. The tipping point comes when the weight leaves your feet and the harness at your waist takes the strain. That is the moment of vulnerability: the moment you place your life on the line and find out whether the system holds.

It does, and I walk down the slate face, feeding the rope slowly through my belay device, dropping down to the next ledge, where a large goat willow spreads its downy-grey boughs. On this whole journey through the shattered mountain interior we have met so few trees that this individual is striking. Peculiar, even. The willow seems so out of place that it gains an aura of personhood that tugs at the roots of some old Welsh folklore. Gwydion comes to mind, the mischievous sorcerer who was forced to assume different animal forms – stag, sow and wolf – as punishment for his wrongdoings. Later, this legendary character animated an entire forest, calling up individual species of alder, oak, aspen, bluebell and holly to rise as warriors and fight in the Cad Goddeu, the Battle of the Trees. I had forgotten how animated the Welsh landscape is; how the mytho-poetic stories live on in these hills and valleys where the language is still spoken.

Down, down, down. Another abseil and a series of ladders lead us further into the base of the pit, where we stand at the bottom of the Lost World, hidden deep inside Elidir Fawr. The air is sombre and deathly still. Suddenly, I feel very tired.

In Nan Shepherd's explorations of the Cairngorms, she writes about 'walking out of my body and into the mountain'.[21] That Zen Buddhist philosophy has always chimed with me and I've sought out those moments in the hills or on the rock, where the self feels a little less solid, a little more fluid, part of something bigger . . . inside a mountain.

For Shepherd, entering a mountain is a slow process of becoming, of allowing the self to soften and mingle into the environment. Here, in Dinorwig, I stand, quite literally, inside a mountain. In the space above my head, millions of tonnes of Elidir Fawr have been removed. I am inside a mountain and can see its inner workings.

There is something medical about this rare internal viewing. The quarrymen's work is like that of the surgeon who cuts through skin and flesh to open up bodies and explore the innermost matter. At first instinct, Dinorwig appears to be a post-mortem: an abandoned industrial waste-land; the ruins of a savaged mountain. But the cutting work was performed on a living body that, while altered, remains very much alive. I think of Frankenstein – then recoil. That is not the right narrative for this place. In Mary Shelley's novel, Frankenstein's monster is the product of nineteenth-century experimentation; a cobbled-together approximation of a human that becomes a bitter outcast who is feared, shunned, hated and pursued. While Dinorwig is a troubling place with a difficult past, the quarry is not hated. The capitalists might have moved on, abandoning the site to go and extract resources from other landscapes using other human bodies; but in Dinorwig, life continues. Every weekend, scores of climbers pour in from across the country and every day locals walk, run and play in the spaces that fathers, brothers, uncles, grandfathers and great-grandfathers worked into existence.

Climbing in Dinorwig, the dizzying scale of waste, absence and industrial transformation is striking; but I am also moved by the beauty that lies within. Mesmerising colours appear out of nowhere. The slate is not just grey or black. It is also teal, mauve, olive, turquoise, caramel, lilac and scarlet. Strange shapes and patterns draw the eye in. In the lines and tones of one wall, I see a William Blake vision – an etching of the human body, a powerful composition of leanest sinew and muscle. For the climber, the towering walls, searing slabs and dark overhangs suggest an infinite range of physical sequences. These sharp features that were dug out of the mountain and sculpted by man invite us to think differently. To move with this rock, we must perform bold and experimental movements.

In opening the body of Elidir Fawr, the quarrymen exposed aeons of time and deep earthly processes. The wrinkles in the slate help us to imagine ancient movements – the laying-down of sediments in long-lost seas and oceans, the collision and division of continents – vast visions well beyond our normal scales of reckoning. Their expert work with this sharp, friable and unforgiving medium produced luminous pieces of compelling insight. The climbers who followed in their footsteps have always had a good grasp of the workmanship that went into these walls. Joe Brown was the first on after the gates closed in 1969, kick-starting the new movement of slate craftsmanship with Opening Gambit. During the mass unemployment of the 1980s, hundreds more climbers piled into the quarry, producing a glut of new lines, including Johnny Dawes' electrifying masterpiece, the Quarryman.

On Rainbow Slab, a gorgeous sheet of coloured slate that looks out over Llyn Peris, a rainbow ripples across the smooth rock face – a giant three-dimensional fold that illustrates where the ancient seabed was pressed and buckled by the force of tectonic-scale movement. On this face, if you can maintain the constant body tension required to stay on tiny edges and little finger pockets, then you can pull up, moving through compressed layers of geological time to stand on top of a rainbow.

VIII

MORAY

SANDSTONE

Lifting my feet from the pebble shingles, I begin to navigate the sandstone corner. Moving up and to the right, cracks for my hands become holds for my feet. I lean in and remove a hand, taking a bunch of nuts from my harness, selecting the right size, slotting the piece into a crack and jiggling until I am confident that it will stay. The nut holds. I attach a quickdraw, clip the rope in, and continue climbing.

Lower down, the rock is slightly damp and sandy. Grit clings to my skin, creating an uncomfortable distance, a faint sliding sensation between fingers and stone. I wipe my hands on my trousers.

I move out onto the arête. Here, at the sharp edge between the enclave and a steep slab, the space around me widens. My heart flutters. Breathing steadily, I let my fingers think. Two cracks run down the wall, on either side of the arête. My right hand sits in comfortably, fingers immersed, knuckles wedged.

Reaching the overlap, I slot some gear into a crack just above my head and pause to consider the next move. This is the bold move – a step out of the corner, around the arête and onto the slab. The angle is overhanging: I must haul myself up and over.

The rock is generous and a large spine hangs at just the right place. I push up with my feet and grasp the feature with first one then two hands. Now I have pulled up and over, and the climb is pretty much done. I scramble up a gentle stone ramp into the dunes, smiling, dragging the rope as I reach for the metal stake, throw a sling around it, secure myself and shout to my partner, 'Safe.'

I have just climbed Stegosaurus, a ten-metre gem at Cummingston.

—

The cliffs at Cummingston overlook the Moray Firth. Picture this vast inlet as an arrowhead that cuts into northern Scotland. Along one edge are Caithness and Sutherland and along the other are Moray and Aberdeenshire. Inverness lies at the arrow tip, some thirty miles southwest of Cummingston. I had never heard of Moray before I moved up to the Highlands. I knew of Inverness, which was up in the distant north and therefore, I assumed, must be cold and grey.

I began climbing regularly on the Moray coast when I moved to Scotland in August 2017. After three years of intense study and focus on one project, I was ready for a new adventure. I wanted to learn more about ecology, conservation and mountain environments. A job came up with the Cairngorms National Park Authority, focused on making opportunities for young people to engage with the national park. I met the person spec and the pay was good so I sent in an application and took a six-hour train ride north for the interview. The following week, they called to offer me the job. I was delighted and terrified. It was a big move but I needed the money and was guaranteed adventure.

Moving up, I knew just two people in the area. One was a climber, who had a busy job as an outdoor instructor, and the other was a walker. I needed to meet people and needed to climb, so I looked for a club, but there were none in the immediate vicinity. Aviemore, Grantown and Kingussie are home to many outdoor instructors and families – people who are often out on the hills and have ready access to a network of eager companions. They don't need a club. The nearest was Moray Mountaineering Club, who meet every Wednesday evening in the summer to climb at Cummingston.

A forty-five-minute drive north after work through pine forests, across moorland, and down into the farmland of Moray brought me to Cummingston. This being Scotland, I knew to expect midges and rain. Sure enough, I arrived to torrential rain. I sat there for five minutes, listening to it hammering on the car roof, watching huge drops cloud the windscreen, wondering what I was going to do. The other climbers lived locally – had they seen the rain and headed to the indoor wall at Elgin? I didn't have anyone's number. I couldn't check. Then it stopped. A climber emerged from the van next to me. I leaped out.

'Are you part of Moray Mountaineering Club?'

'Yeh.'

'I'm new to the club. Will the others have gone down to Elgin since it's raining?'

'Nah, we're early yet.'

'It's not too wet?'

'No. Some of the rock will be dry and the rest dries fast.'

He shouldered a boulder mat; I grabbed my rucksack and followed him down to the crags.

We passed banks bursting with grass and wildflowers, all fresh and gasping after the downpour. Pink-white petals of dog rose hung from prickly arched stems, mingling with bramble, nettle, grass and docks. Sea pink waved on long stems alongside red campion and stout yellow ragwort. Vetch tendrils and lacy white cow parsley added to the jumble of colour and scent. My companion didn't speak much. Tall and thin, he had the aloof air of a Serious Climber. When the bank fell away to our right, the sea appeared. We stood above a small bay – a beach of grey shingle and rock-pool reefs – lined by cliffs, perhaps ten or fifteen metres high. The climber led the way down a rough path of muddy sand worn deep into the grass. Bypassing the beach, he clambered over boulders to reach the foot of the cliffs.

'The others will show up in a bit.'

He went off to boulder some hard problem and I left him to it.

Waiting for the rest of the club to arrive, I poked around. The cliffs formed exquisite sculptured shapes. Erosion by sea, wind and rain had smoothed, rounded and loosened fracture lines. Great stacks rose from rock pools like the tottering turrets of a sandcastle slipping away into the sea. Above the sea-smoothed base, the stacks jutted out in craggy overhangs. In a corner of the cliffs, I found an opening and shuffled through a low passageway in the rock. After a few cramped, dark metres, I emerged into a vast space. Wings clattered as pigeons leaped from their perches, escaping up to the light through a great hole in the ceiling. Curved archways looked out on the sea while shingle and boulders banked up towards the back wall. The roof was curved and scalloped, cracked and lined in a mesmerising form licked out by the sea. I had stumbled into a damp cathedral.

Looking up with my climber's eyes, I saw inviting edges. Ten metres off the ground there was a prominent lip which I felt with my mind's eye. The hold looked generous: my hands could confidently grasp that rock, my arms could comfortably lock off; I could hang. Where would I put my feet? How would I get up there? Climbing makes me question the rock, looking for passages. I scanned the surrounding rock, looking for a route up to the lip. The best option was to follow a steep, curving overhang. I shuddered. The moves looked impossible. The lip remained a flight of fancy.

While my eyes roamed and marvelled, my hands itched. My fingers wanted to grasp, to cling, to hold, to feel. I grew impatient and turned my attention to more accessible rock. Perhaps a low-level traverse would be possible. I left the cave and joined the cliffs, following ledges trending leftwards, keeping my feet off the ground, careful not to climb too high. When the feet became delicate, I sought solid handholds. Here was a hidden bowl – my left hand plunged in, relaxing into a strong grip. Now the feet improved and my toes stepped comfortably along a wide ledge. Then the hands became more difficult. Sharp edges smoothed out into rounded domes and slopers. I moved my hips in to the rock, activating a new source of stability. My body warmed, muscles heating with the tension. I reached left – and found a ceramic cup rim. My fingers grasped this feature gratefully, and my body swung to hang underneath, feet resting in a couple of curved scallops. I looked left – from here the rock became more overhanging and the features less generous. Enough. My feet landed on the shingle with a dull clunk.

———

Over the next few weeks and months, I enjoyed getting to know the club. They were a friendly mix of teachers, postmen, foresters and engineers. On the Wednesday evening meets at Cummingston, there were generally around ten of us, sometimes more, sometimes less. There was another section of Moray Mountaineering Club that I never met – the group who went on the Bus Meets – weekend trips to walk the hills. Since I had a car and was happy walking alone, I felt no need to meet this group. Of the Wednesday night group, most were trad climbers, although some also bouldered, disappearing off to home in on hard moves, armed with chalk and bouldering mats. There was probably a climber from every decade of life, from a couple of us in our twenties through to a guy in his seventies. Alfie, a friendly golden retriever, barked from the rock pools when he wanted stones thrown.

I loved getting to know this rock. My year in the Lake District had shown me how something approaching a familial relationship can develop between climbers and their local crags. Returning to revisit and rework the same patch of rock, you soon learn its nooks and crannies and become conversant with its many lines and aspects. Then you come again and notice something new, for the crag changes in different weathers and so does your relationship to it. There are times when you are strong and you chase the harder lines – and other points in the season where you stick to more accommodating stretches. Spending many hours at that same crag, including all the time when you are not climbing – just talking, sitting, watching or belaying – brings the ambience further in, writing the nature of that spot into your personal geography.

The Moray crags do not have the drama of some sea cliffs, where you abseil in to a small stance above surging waves and follow long, steep lines with heart-stopping exposure. The Moray sea cliffs are gentler and have their own charm. The sandstone is a warm ochre, a mixed palette of beiges, yellows, oranges, greys and browns. At high tide, the sea washes the foot of some sections. Here the rock wears a lurid green fringe. Higher up, the stone is bleached grey. Orange scars mark the places where blocks have fallen out. Lichens colonise surfaces that are not disturbed by climbers, spreading white splodges, egg-yolk bloomings and crisp green tendrils. The stone has plenty of character. There are pocked faces that look like an old tree, pitted with insect holes. In other places the patterns resemble Aboriginal artwork. Overhanging corners gape. Faint shadows show gentle scallop curves. The rock strata holds stripes, lines and herringbone patterns. Lattices cut across the system. Wind and water have deepened the features into cracks, grooves, ledges and blocks. Here the stone is scored as though someone has marked it with a deep cross.

The stone has superb friction. On a cold day, I placed a gloved hand on the rock. I slowly peeled it away, delighting in the gentle Velcro action, as fibres caught and clung to the surface, before the pressure grew too strong and they sprang back to my glove with a gentle tearing sound. Without gloves, I felt the grain of the rock. Rough but not sharp, the fine texture lets skin meld into stone. This permeability is not imagined. The sandstone also absorbs water. When the air is thick with humidity, sheltered enclaves can feel like damp, sandy beach towels. Generally though, barefoot or in rubber-soled shoes, my feet stuck to the rock. The texture invites trust.

Geologists call this particular rock the Hopeman Sandstone Formation. It was formed around 250 million years ago, somewhere between the end of the Permian and the start of the Triassic Period, when all the continents were clumped together in a supercontinent called Pangea. The climate was hot and arid, producing extensive deserts like the present-day Sahara. Wind blew the sand into shifting dunes and pressure lithified the sediments into sandstone. In the National Museum of Scotland, a chunk of Hopeman Sandstone is on display. Shaped like a giant pizza shovel, the rock is rippled like the sand in a shallow bay where water flows and furrows. Grease from many hands has smoothed the gritty surface. Looking closely when I visited, I saw a crescent-shaped indent disrupting the ripples. My palm rested comfortably within the oval dish, my fingers reached into a faint series of indents. The footprint was left by a reptile. The creature padded over this stone when it was still sand some 250 million years ago. There is another trail of footprints hidden in the back of a cave at Cummingston. Climbers who had been exploring the rock for twenty years did not know the prints existed until a geologist pointed them out one day. In this dark corner, I reach my hand up to a smooth roof and feel the imprints on the low ceiling. Once again, my palm fits perfectly within the dimple. My thoughts fly back to the National Museum, recalling that set of partnering prints.

In the dimly lit basement of the museum, another lump of Hopeman sandstone is safely stowed behind glass. Below the pitted ridge at the top of the stone there is a series of curved indents, as though someone has dragged lines through clay. The impression is clear: these hollows formed around bones. The rock displays an ancient spine and ribcage that belonged to a *Gordonia*, a genus of reptile that lived through the Late Permian and Early Triassic periods. Other fossil findings revealed that *Gordonia* were herbivores that had two tusks in their upper jaws but no teeth. *Gordonia* chewed plants like a turtle – shearing their jaws backwards and forwards to break apart tough leaves and stems. The ribcage in the stone is a similar size to mine: perhaps this creature was about the same size as me. It is strange to think that as I climbed the Moray sea cliffs, beneath my fingertips there will have been other remains like this, fossilised and entombed for millions of years. Like a pond skater, I darted across the surface, barely touching the depths.

I am not the only one to value the surface of this stone. Hopeman Sandstone, quarried at Clashach, is shipped (at great expense) to provide cladding for high-status buildings around the world. The roll-call includes La Sagrada Família in Barcelona and the 9/11 memorial in New York. Closer to home, a number of buildings in Edinburgh use the stone, including the castle, Scottish Parliament, and the National Museum of Scotland. I was curious. What does the rock look like in an urban context? Why do architects incorporate it into statement building projects? Walking down George IV Bridge in Edinburgh, I weaved through hordes of tourists taking in the sights. A gaggle of Spanish school pupils approached a café where a couple stood, arms linked, beaming across the pavement at seven smartphone cameras clutched by seven middle-aged Asian women. The café is said to be the birthplace of Harry Potter. I dodged onto the road, avoiding J.K. Rowling's magic touch. Ahead, on the left, sandstone cliffs reared up – or is this a castle? A round turret sits at one end. The walls are pink, ochre, beige and rust, like a warm day at the seaside. The stone is cut and polished into smooth, regular blocks. The dressing shows off the markings within the rock. There are splodges, stripes and spots. Patterns like animal print. A fine brown line divides a beige block. Some panels are marbled, as if the stone were a sheet of paper, dipped in ink swirled on water. My palm slid across the cool surface. The sun came out and, for a moment, the blocks glittered.

It was strange to see the stone that I was so intimately familiar with dressed up for this bold statement of cosmopolitan modernity – the aforementioned National Museum of Scotland. The facade is impressive – but I couldn't climb these walls. Or perhaps I could if I took a hammer and chisel with me and knocked some texture back into the rock.

——

On the Moray cliffs, the weathered forms have a distinctly different feel. The craggy structure allows for a range of intricate movements. The shapes are not always dignified or impressive. Per Rectum is a case in point. This memorable climb navigates some peculiar and varied rock features. The bottom few feet are weedy and slippery – the route starts at the tideline. From there, you climb into the dark, curving sweep of a large bowl like the inside of a wave, moving up a great crackline between one section of cliff and another. To exit the bowl, you must ascend the wall of the wave to the crest, which forms a great overhanging roof, where you can squeeze through the gap between the cliffs. Making things a little more complicated, there is a block jammed in this gap, creating a small hole to squeeze through, perhaps thirty centimetres wide and fifty centimetres long.

Working my way up to a shelf just under the hole, I reached my hands up onto the surfaces above. So far so good. I pulled up, my head emerged and I could see the sea again as I looked out over a wide ledge (the halfway point of the route). However, my lower body didn't follow my head and shoulders. It wouldn't fit through the hole. I tried again, pulling harder. My hips got stuck. I tried a third time. No good. My hips were at the wrong angle. I needed to rotate them slightly to fit through the opening. Simple enough, but the shelf I was using for my foot forced my hips into this particular angle. To move my hips, I needed to move my feet and, with my body filling the hole, I couldn't see where else my toes could go. After a great deal of fumbling, hip jiggling, knee twisting and swearing, eventually I found the right position, and my hips squeezed through.

This technique is called thrutching. Thrutch. Say it. The word sits heavily, catching at the sides of your mouth like a climber in a tight spot. This Anglo-Saxon word lingered around in northern dialect before climbers seized it. My grandmother (a Lancashire woman with a passion for words and language) would say, 'Eee we were fair thrutched up' to describe a workplace where you are up to your elbows in clutter. (Think of an office where cups and stationery and long-forgotten Secret Santa gifts crowd any space left between towering heaps of books, folders and papers.) In the climbing world, 'thrutch' is a verb, capturing a particular style of movement with onomatopoeic precision. There is nothing elegant in a thrutch. You squeeze, twist, pull, push and press, squirming your body against one edge and then another, trying to make your way through the awkward spot, one centimetre at a time. Like those adverts where people desperately try to squeeze into a pair of jeans three sizes too small, the human body becomes awkward, undignified and hilarious. In these situations, a spectator is in the best position to appreciate the entertainment. The poor soul who is grappling with their bodily limitations tends to be otherwise occupied. A climber cannot laugh while thrutching. For one thing, the sudden expansion and contraction of your rib cage and stomach would increase the challenge. For another, generally, the harder the thrutch, the more exasperated and irritated the thrutcher becomes.

Afterwards, I sat at the top of Per Rectum, my legs dangling over the edge, belaying my partner up the route. I had not climbed with him before. He was one of the older climbers within the club and he hadn't climbed for a while. He got to the hole and I held the rope. His head and arms emerged; his legs remained below. He cursed and muttered, squeezed and pushed, all without much success. Time passed. He kept trying. The name of the climb flashed across my mind. The corners of my mouth twitched. I didn't know him well enough to make the joke. I looked out to sea to regain my composure. Eventually, he gave up his thrutching. I lowered him down, and someone else followed me up.

—

After my first rain-soaked visit to Cummingston, I returned often. I discovered a pleasant microclimate that the locals refer to as the Moray Med. The weather is often drier, warmer and sunnier than the mountains, and even the land nearby that is only slightly further inland. Putting the analogy to the test, I brought my swimming things along on my second visit. When I had finished climbing for the evening, I changed and slid into the water. While the evening air was smooth as velvet, the water was painfully refreshing. More Baltic than Mediterranean.

On the long Scottish summer days, the evenings stretched out indefinitely. The light was at once rich and delicate, having a peculiar distilled clarity that was both soft and intense. Sitting and belaying at the top of the cliffs, looking out over the sea in the gentlest of dusks, the glimmering water seemed to caress my skin. Away to the north, Morven stood out in a shapely triangle, like a child's mountain sketch. When the sun set over Ben Wyvis, the mountain disappeared into light. Rain showers came and went, passing along the firth. These distant grey curtains held the light: luminous rain briefly obscured patches of sea, hill and oil rig. Sometimes the rain caught us. If it came in heavy, we stashed our ropes and bags in enclaves under the rock and rushed to hide in the cave. Once the rain had moved on, we went back to the rock. With its rough veneer, the stone still gripped, but the water brought out the sand, making the surface soft and gritty.

When the clocks changed, the club shifted to climb indoors at an old church in Elgin. This was good practise, keeping up my fitness and getting me out of the house on dark evenings, when I would otherwise have drawn the curtains and hidden under a duvet or two. But the drive to Elgin was long and dark. I couldn't wait for the return of daylight and warmer weather, so I could pick up where I had left off on the rock. However, the following summer was destined to be different. Just as the days were lengthening and the snow was melting, I lost my grounding. The relationship that I had been in for years came to an end. I suddenly felt like a rock, far out to sea. After the initial storm, waves of grief washed over me all summer. The pain was not constant; it surged and fell like the tides. Gnawing agony gave way to ebbing numbness; at low tide a window briefly opened, before the waters began to rise once again.

Within this churning sea of change and loss, climbing became essential. Some people turn to drink, I relaxed on the rock. My restlessness found relief in physical movement. Pulling up cliffs set the heart beating, forcing the blood to flow faster around my clamouring muscles and so the body loosened through strenuous activity. Questions, doubts, fears and uncertainties fell quiet: climbing made my mind focus on the world at my fingertips. Previously I had sought many things from climbing – company, achievement, fun, adventure, exercise. Now these ends became less important. My motivation was stripped back. I did not expect to enjoy myself. I was not there to prove anything. That summer, I sought total immersion. In the vertical space between the ground and the top of the route, everything else fell away. I sank into the rock.

Through this changed approach, something crystallised. I began to lead-climb with greater confidence. Previously, when I moved above my gear on unfamiliar rock, I met my ego and two conflicting impulses. The ego wanted me to perform well; it also wanted me to stay safe. Climbs could be torturous. An internal chatter of self-doubt might set in (*Should I do this move? Can I do this climb? What if I can't?*) Reaching a hard move, I became embroiled in a battle between performance and self-preservation. In these circumstances I backed off many climbs, self-esteem in tatters. But that summer, shock and grief had shattered my ego. I came to the rock with a new openness. I climbed purely to be with the rock and discovered that lead climbing brought me in closer. Climbing at the sharp end of the rope, route-finding and placing protection demanded greater focus, and that was exactly what I needed.

My climbing progressed. I moved on from climbing VS and became comfortable leading HVS. The next step was to try an E1. I have not said anything on grading, but in climbing, every route is given a grade which, in theory, gives climbers some idea of the difficulty of the undertaking. Indoor walls and bolted routes use the French system – a simple set of numerical grades that runs from 1 to 9. The trad grading system is more analogue, using a combination of adjectives and numbers. The adjectives begin at Moderate. After that comes Difficult and then Very Difficult. Then come the Severes, of which there are Mild Severes, Very Severes, Mild Very Severes and Hard Very Severes. Confused yet? When things get harder still, they become Extremely Severe, at which point the climbers ran out of adverbs and adjectives and added numbers, so an E1 is the easiest of the Extremely Severe scale, which currently runs up to an E11.

Alongside the adjectives, trad routes are also given a numerical technical grade, for example a VS 4a or an E1 5b. (Naturally, the British trad technical number does not align with the French numbers.) The whole system takes some getting your head around and is yet another one of those aspects of trad climbing that can only really be grasped through experience. What seems convoluted and unnecessarily complicated at first gradually begins to make sense. The pairing of adjectives and numbers opens up a space for the nuance and variables of traditional climbing, which is always a balance between technical difficulty and gear. How hard are the moves and how safe will I be when I perform them?

One Sunday afternoon in July, the opportunity to try something harder arrived. I headed to Covesea, a few kilometres east along the coast from Cummingston, to climb with Ben, who was good company on the rock: chatty, enthusiastic, with a sharp eye for wildlife. We climbed similar grades and so became reliable climbing partners. At Covesea, we walked into the crags past the scorched remains of a gorse field. The summer was hot and dry: fire quickly took hold of gorse, heather, grass or woodland. The fire services were kept busy. At the white hexagonal coastguard tower we turned right, picking our way along narrow brambled paths on the clifftops. The descent is a little more treacherous than at Cummingston. We found the right turn-off and came to a small cleft between the cliffs called the Lummie. At the top of this narrow chimney, five rough steps have been formed by stones wedged into the gap. Where the steps end, the rock falls away and the chimney widens. A rope ladder hangs from a rusting iron peg. I grabbed on, awkwardly swinging, feeling my body and rucksack weighing heavily on the rope, my feet struggling to find the wooden rungs as the ladder twisted and swung. At the top of the Lummie I stood in sunshine, breathing in the thick, sweet scent of gorse; inside the chimney, the air was cool and damp, the smell of the sea rising to meet me. The transition is sharp. I was relieved to tumble out onto the boulder beach below.

The tide was out and we did some great routes. I belayed Ben for an age while he figured out Protection Racket (E1 5b), a route with a large overhanging roof that proved difficult to climb out from. He tried various combinations, his legs flailing through space as his feet struggled to find purchase on the overhanging roof. Meanwhile, his hands sought the key that would enable him to pull up and over. He took a fall, his gear held, and he swung. He tried again, persistently hunting – then he found the hold, cracked the combination, and completed the route.

Round the corner, in Boulders Bay, I led Annie Hall (HVS 5a), a steep vertical crack that cuts through the latticed lines in the sandstone. I had had my eye on this route for a few weeks. The name appealed to me. I like the character Annie Hall in Woody Allen's film – her style, her gawkiness and her distinctive masculine-femininity. Her ambiguous place somewhere between conventional gender roles struck a chord.

The gender space of climbing can be peculiar. Media often homes in on the risk, ego and adrenaline aspects of the sport, making it appear, to outsiders, a particularly macho pastime. Historically, the sport was male-dominated and many of the published accounts of climbing are by men. But on the rock – away from the books and history and external views – many gender differences fall away. With my gear, harness and ropes on, I feel much more fluid. And the partnership at the heart of the activity can enable deep respectful friendships to develop between the sexes.

There are still moments, though, when I feel a touch of loneliness at the crags. More and more women are becoming climbers, helping to balance the books, but the spread varies across the disciplines. Indoor climbing, bouldering and sport climbing draw in more women than traditional climbing, which requires more equipment and a wider set of technical skills. Geography also plays a role. Certain regions have more women climbers than others. I had landed in a place where I met few female trad climbers.

That sense of being outnumbered was not helped by the route names at Covesea. Since most first ascents have been done by men, climbs are seldom named by women, and this is where the historic masculinity of the sport can intrude at the crag. A sample of names at Covesea includes Thatcher's Crack, Special Brew, Fascist Octopus, Fascist Republic and Urban Gorilla. Fairly innocuous. But there are worse. Horny Beast, Legover Wall, Battle of the Bulge and Primitive Thoughts about Modern Girls.[22] Within such a library, Annie Hall stood out. Unlike all those names that gestured to a humour and sensibility that was far from my own, here was a route that I felt could be *my* route. I identified with it in a way I have never really done with a climb before or since.

There was a certain trepidation. The route did not look soft. The steep angle and dynamic start suggested a sustained challenge. To do the route justice, I did not want to second it, following someone else up, safe on a rope from above. I wanted to lead Annie Hall clean, finding the holds, gear and movements for myself. That Sunday afternoon, I went for it.

Stood on tiptoes among the coloured beach pebbles and strands of black bladderwrack, I stretched up, reaching around for a generous pair of hand holds. The sea had eaten away the bottom of the cliff, leaving a dark gaping void below the wall. The first foot placement was at chest height. This was a big opening move.

But once I had made it onto the face, there would be lots of features to work with. The lower section was full of natural iron deposits which, like rivets driven into the rock, formed neat little round nodules. In other places, the iron had melded with the craggy sculpted sandstone to produce sharp rusted features that dripped from the wall like the hulk of a shipwreck.

Pull up and believe.

I reached up and heaved onto the wall, foot swinging onto the high ledge while all the metalware hanging from my harness jangled. Now moving into a standing position, my hands grappled for something higher, arms wrapped around a ledge, hips moving back into balance – I leaned in and paused, hugging into the sandy-iron stone, breathing.

Below a tuft of sea spleenwort, a scoop welcomed the big red hex which wedged in, steadfast.

Gear placed, I moved on again, following the sequence of the piece as it flowed in and out over a series of bulges on intricately sculpted sandstone. Bubbles, pockets, holes and dimples were circled by sharp crests, lips and soft rims. The cross-bedding had produced defined lines and layers while erosion had opened out a jumble of concavities and convexities. Moving up and around the stonescape, I enjoyed peering into the cracks and holes, feeling that rush of privilege from the magical perspective that climbing enables.

But the flakey details also begged questions. Ben mentioned

loose rock at the top. Banging and shaking, I tested things before trusting.

At the lichen zone, the wall came alive with crispy tufts and branches of *Ramalina siliquosa* – sea ivory. Looking down to place my feet, I could see exactly where previous climbers had stood. Their footprints had made a lasting impression on the green ledges.

The wall steepened and I paused again where the two cracks ran together, meeting in a small, dark, blocky over-hang. Taking one arm off, I reached across my body, fumbling through the metalware hanging from my waist, seeking out the right cam. The gold one slotted into a gap between blocks. It sat – but didn't feel right. The intricate nature of this rock makes protection difficult. Gear moves and walks. Scanning around, I found another space: a crack where a gold nut sat tight. Now secure, I braced for the last few strenuous moves.

Pulling through the overhang – feet placed with care, legs pushing to support the arms – I moved into the final upper reaches where the rocks turned smoother. With less to grasp, I pressed with care, watching for choss as my eyeline drew level with the grassy top and a powerful scent rose to me. Guano. I had reached a favoured gull perch. Mantling up and over, my nose briefly drew in unbearably close to the heavily fertilised ground before I scrambled upright again. I had done it.

Looking down as I sorted the ropes to bring Ben up to join me, I noticed a scarlet hole gleaming on my index finger. Annie Hall had broken the skin.

Opposite to Annie Hall is another wall of colder white and grey rock that overlooks the sea. This one does not have intricate craggy details: it is tall, smooth and steep. Like a chessboard, that vast face is faintly scored with irregular squares and oblongs. In the bottom left corner, a few squares are missing where immense blocks have fallen out, creating a long, dark, overhanging roof. The routes on this face are harder. The easiest is Banana Republic (E1 5b). Flushed by my success on Annie Hall, I now considered this route. I hadn't climbed Banana Republic before, but I had seen other people on it. It looked difficult, but it also looked possible. I needed a new challenge.

This was perhaps not the best day for me to try leading an E1. I was not exactly prepared. I was hungover. I had been at a wedding the day before which had led into a long ceilidh session in a village hall. While belaying, standing on the beach or sitting on the clifftops, I looked out to sea, feeling distant and hollow. But I knew that climbing would help to bring me back, forcing mind and body to become present again, lifting my heavy mood. That afternoon, I figured I wanted to climb an E1, so why not try now?

I tied in and began again. The first third of Banana Republic was straightforward. I balanced and bridged, pushing up small in-cuts in the corner towards the roof, which lurked, dark and ominous, overhead. As my helmet bumped up against the rocky ceiling, I shifted my feet around, hunting a comfortable stance to breathe and place some protection.

Erring on the side of caution, I placed a cam and a nut. This pleased Ben, who sometimes commented on my bold approach to protection. (Bold, in climbing-speak, means climbing with little protection. That style of mine was a hangover from the Yorkshire gritstone days when I had learned to lead with limited equipment and no cams.) Then it was time to move out from under the roof, hauling myself up and over onto the open wall above. I was nervous. I was comfortable in the roof, I knew the rock, the holds and the gear; the next move was a step into the unknown. Would good holds come? When would I next get some gear? How sustained and strenuous would the next section be?

I moved up, pressing down hard with my toes onto a notch no wider than a five-pence coin, fingers grappling with an awkward crack in the wall above. I saw a ledge with a faint dusting of white chalk. That must be the next handhold. It was just out of reach. I climbed back down into the nook, paused, shook the tension out of my arms and tried again. The ledge remained beyond my grasp. I retreated, returning to the enclave like an insect scuttling in and out of its home in one of the sandy holes on these cliffs.

The next time, I tried to move boldly – pushing and reaching with dynamism – but still I couldn't quite make the ledge. This rock was so demanding. All of the tension and effort were wearing on me. My forearms were screaming, legs shaking, palms sweaty, energy draining fast. I had lost the strength to down-climb. So I let go.

In that moment, time expands. The mind races to the gear nestled in the cracks below: will it hold? Will the rope catch? How far will I fall? The gap between letting go and being held feels epic. Milliseconds passed – and my harness cut tight into my waist. The gear held and I swung on the rope, heart beating fast. All the moisture in my mouth had disappeared and my forearms were set hard as concrete. The move required a powerful commitment; I had lacked confidence. Finally, I backed off and Ben lowered me down. He had agreed in advance that he would finish the route if I couldn't. He took the gear from my harness and headed up, taking his time, cursing a little and powering through the section I had struggled with. I followed him up and was glad I hadn't gone any further. The steep wall remained steep, the holds were smaller and more infrequent than I would like, my arm muscles screamed. We exchanged some 'thank fuck that's over' comments and agreed we'd climbed enough.

The day was still young though, so before we refreshed ourselves with a pint, we set off to find an old millstone and cave hidden further along the shore. Leaving our bags at the stone steps, we picked our way further along the shore, hopping across boulders, crunching shingle and sliding through bladderwrack. Ben slowed to hunt in the rock pools.

'It's around here somewhere . . .'

There, in among scattered sandstone blocks and sea-rounded stones, was a flat-topped circular form. In the centre of the stone, a round hole pooled water. Below the blue-sky reflections were seaweeds, shells, and the smooth red blob of a sea anemone. The millstone was incomplete: the hole had not been drilled right through. Something must have gone wrong. The outer circle was rough – one of the edges looked as though an extra chunk had been knocked off. Perhaps the workman messed up. Maybe the stone proved unexpectedly awkward.

We continued around the headland and came to a small bay where the cliffs curved around a shingle beach. At the foot of the ochre cliffs was a small dark opening, with what looked like a door in it. We left the beach and followed a thin path up grassy slopes to the entrance of Sculptor's Cave. The sea must once have been higher than it is today – the cave was formed by the sea, but now it sits metres above the shoreline. There are two entrance passageways. The right one is boarded up with sun-bleached plywood. Someone has fashioned a crude window into the boarding, letting light spill into the black interior.

We entered the left passage, our eyes picking out markings in the soft desert rock. Haphazard graffiti spells names, initials and dates. Someone has spray-painted a neat white anarchist sign. Higher up, 'Peace' is scratched into the stone. Further into the gloom, where the yellow rock is moulded dark green, we found older markings:

W ENDING
12 of MAR 169_
CURSED BE THEY Yt HINDER

Who was the curse for? Is 'W ENDING' a name? William Ending? Was he the curser or the cursed? Or do those letters make the curse eternal, WITHOUT ENDING? The 1690s were a time of great political unrest, of strife between Catholics and Protestants and Jacobite rebellions. In this dark space, a curse could linger, semi-hidden, undisturbed for centuries.

The carvings go back further. Looking more closely, crude shapes are etched into the surface. An upright salmon outline appears next to a crescent and V-rod. Near the ceiling are two pentagrams. Three shapes like the arch of a whale jawbone stand together. Each pointed arc is slightly larger than the palm of my hand: a triple oval. Elsewhere, there is a flower and mirror, a disc and rectangle. These are Pictish symbols, engraved some time in the sixth or seventh century CE. At one time, the Picts were a powerful presence in northeast Scotland.

Burghead Fort is a few miles along the coast. This was once the power centre of the Pictish kingdom. The fort sits on an exposed promontory at the edge of land and sea, making use of a natural vantage point. Traces of Pictish language also linger in the northeast. When I moved up, I was surprised and pleased to find familiar Welsh-sounding place names: Abernethy, Aberlour, Aberdeen. Like Aberystwyth and Abergavenny, these Scottish settlements are located at river mouths. 'Aber' was the Pictish word for a river mouth or confluence, suggesting that the Pictish language was perhaps closer to Welsh (P-Celtic) than Gaelic (Q-Celtic).[23] Yet despite these marks in the land, little is known about the Picts. They did not keep written records or develop a recognisable alphabet. Their symbol stones – found across northeast Scotland – provide clues to their life and culture, but we cannot be sure what the symbols mean. Some think that the carvings of birds, animals and other shapes were territorial markers; others suggest they commemorated particular people or important events.

In this cave, the human trail goes back even further. Archaeological excavations into the earth below my feet uncovered Viking, Roman, Iron Age and Bronze Age objects from as far back as 1200 BCE. There are amber beads and Roman coins, pieces of pottery, tools made from bone, a pair of iron tweezers. The cave may have been used for metallurgy at some point. Slag, ironwork, charcoal and ash were found among the debris. Other caves along the coast have been lived in. A friend showed me black and white photographs of her family camped out in one of the caves. They were travellers who moved around northeast Scotland, finding work where they could. But Sculptor's Cave was never lived in. The objects found here belonged to different peoples and cultures from across a vast time period. Did all these people visit the cave and deposit their objects? Or did the items travel great distances, traded and exchanged between different hands, before they were placed in the cave? We don't know.

Among the objects, many human bones were also found. One cluster dates from the Roman Iron Age, some time around CE 300. In Elgin Museum, three bones are on display. These delicate objects would sit comfortably within the palm of your hand. They are a similar yellowing-brown colour to the Hopeman Sandstone. In the centre of each knobbly triangle is a round hole. This is where the spinal cord once sat. One of the vertebrae has a slight nick taken out of it. The vertebral body of the smallest bone is exposed – a tiny cavity reveals dark pinprick holes. These remains show trauma. In Sculptor's Cave, six young people were decapitated by a sharp iron blade. Was this violence a ritual sacrifice or a brutal incident of tribal warfare? We don't know. As in the 1690s, when a curse was cut into the sandstone walls, the executions took place during a time of great unrest. Invading Roman armies were pushing further north and the Pictish kingdom was forming. Perhaps some of these political, cultural and societal pressures brought people to this cave. Perhaps the space offered some kind of answer if you knew how to ask. Prior to this, there were more bones. During the Late Bronze Age (1200–1000 BCE), human bodies were brought here and left to decompose. Some were then partially retrieved for secondary burials or rituals. This was not a violent practice: for over a millennium, the cave was used as a place for the respectful treatment of the dead. Maybe the cave provided an opening for meaning. It is hard to grasp all of the history held in this dark space. The layers of culture and politics overlap, collide and coexist.

I turned and walked out. Forty paces from the back of the cave, I squinted in broad daylight, relieved to breathe in grass, sea and sky once more. In contrast to the limestone caves in the south of France, where ancient paintings are hidden deep underground, accessed through an extensive network of passages and caverns, Sculptor's Cave is only just tucked away from the beach. Yet the transitions from land to sea, light to dark, air to earth are sharp and unnerving. Perhaps it was the in-between nature of the cave that drew people here, again and again, over thousands of years. Most of the historic matter was not found in the dark interior, but around the entrance passageway. The Pictish carvings are almost in daylight, the bones lay in the entrance, the curse is hidden slightly further in. Cultural activity centred on the liminal space between beach and cave.

An archaeologist speculates that Sculptor's Cave may have been 'an area for people to make contact between this world and another.' I can see how the cave might conjure a sense of contact between different worlds. Outside, there is light and colour. Waves break on the shore, gulls call overhead. The sun warms the skin and the breeze lifts hair. Inside is dark and quiet. The air is still and skin tightens to the cool darkness, which has an earthy-damp feel.

Leaving the cave, I was blinded once again, blinking

rapidly in the brightness. My shoulders relaxed. I moved between two different worlds. The cave has real potency, but I didn't have the cultural practices to engage with its liminal power. Like stepping inside a church or a mosque, I didn't know what to do in the space. I was glad to tumble out, returning to daylight, the sound of the waves and the crunch of shells underfoot.

But later, I reflected that my weekly pilgrimage to the sea cliffs is not so different. Like the inside of Sculptor's Cave, rock climbing produces an intense visceral response. Rock faces are not comfortable. Sometimes my muscles scream and my skin tears; I feel exposed; I get scared. Sometimes I want to come down. The rock puts me in a space where distinct realms open up. Suddenly I am aware of the yawning difference between the start and end of a route. The ground and the wall. Horizontal and vertical planes are felt realities. I try to keep risk and safety in balance. Life and death are no longer abstract. When climbing, these worlds can become tangible with intense immediacy. I do not seek to overcome or deny any of them. The risks are real. Like the Bronze and Iron Age people, I am a human body inside a profound liminal space. The body must adapt. Linear time vanishes; the moment is infinite.

IX

CAIRNGORMS

GRANITE

On my first trip onto the plateau, I stamped across the surface. With each step, twelve metal teeth bit the ice. I had to concentrate to keep each footfall flat and steady so that the crampon points pierced the ice evenly. I was told to walk like John Wayne, keeping my legs apart so that the inch-long metal spikes strapped to my boots did not catch on my trousers, snagging the fabric, making me tumble. I found a rhythm and my eyes wandered. Below us, smoky cloud appeared, swelling and smothering the valleys. Ahead, snow and ice rolled out for kilometres. The plateau shone in bright winter sun.

This was 2008. I was nineteen, discovering the Cairngorms for the first time over New Year with my university mountaineering club on what was also my first ever venture north of the border. Fifteen of us stayed in a mountaineering hut in Newtonmore for a week. Each day we got up in the dark, gulped down porridge and tea, before falling out of the door to get the most of the short winter daylight and bag a few Munros. I had never heard of a Munro before then, but by Friday, after a week in the mountains, trudging through snow to reach small stony cairns, I was crowned champion with eleven peaks under my belt.

I had never known cold like it. Growing up in Wales, cold meant puddles that cracked like crème brûlée. As a child, I gambolled along rutted farm tracks, pausing at frozen puddles where I would tentatively place a foot. Applying light pressure, I watched muddy water bubble up and flow over the ice; with more pressure, the ice broke and I leaped clear before my foot got wet. In exceptional conditions, the puddle had dried away. Then I could stomp with confidence, shattering ice like frosted glass. In the Cairngorms, whole streams were frozen over and icicles hung like curtains from rooftops. Our breath froze to our hair and after a long day on the hill, water bottles began to rattle with ice forming inside. The snow was also different. In Wales, snow was wet. The best was good for sledging or would stick together for snowballs. That week the Cairngorm snow was hard. Sometimes the crust was fragile and I walked lightly, trying to avoid plunging into the depths. The best patches had condensed into a thick snowpack and you could walk across the top.

To navigate this strange new land, I needed a different set of tools. Back home, I used wellies and a sledge (although I had always envied the farmer kids who shot down the hills on old car bonnets). In the Cairngorms, plastic wouldn't cut it. I needed something sharp and strong. I had to learn to use an ice axe and crampons. Crampons, I discovered, were fiddly. The fabric straps that fasten around your boots need to be pulled tight – which is difficult with cold fingers and impossible in mittens. Judging when to put them on was crucial. Best to decide before reaching that steep, icy slope, when stopping to rummage in your rucksack and fasten the metal to your shoes would put you off balance and ready to slip. Whereas crampons are about timing and anticipation, my ice axe became a dependable companion. I kept it in hand as a short walking stick, using the point to provide stability and grip on steep slopes. When the ice hardened, I swung the axe and cut steps to help my boots find purchase.

Early on the trip, we practised ice-axe arrests. Sliding down banks, I thrust the pick in and threw my weight over the axe, leaning into my shoulder and lifting my legs to bring myself to a stop. We shouted and panted our way back up the slope to try again and again, gasping as snow found its way in through gaps in clothing. The game was fun until I realised the gravity of the lesson. Producing an ice-axe arrest as an instinctive reflex could mean the difference between life and death.

On New Year's Eve, we were blessed with exceptional conditions. Leaving before sunrise to make the most of the light, we headed up to the plateau. As we clambered across frozen streams and trudged through the snow beneath the northern corries, the sun rose. Cloud gathered, smothering the valleys, but high on the plateau the atmosphere turned warm and sunny. In the most unlikely of places, we began to peel off layers. The snow held our weight, and we tramped across rolling ice fields to the distant summit of Ben Macdui.

I remember pulling up the final slopes and stopping dead, gasping in the dazzling blue light. We stood on an island in the sky. As far as we could see, in every direction, white peaks rose from an ocean of grey fog. My spirit soared trying to take it all in. I couldn't believe how many mountains there were – all around us – all shining in the sun. The scale was breathtaking. Expanded, we filled with light and space and mountain.

Walking back from Ben Macdui, the sky paled into soft turquoise, tingeing orange at the horizon. Our shadows stretched out. Absurdly long legs and limbs danced in blue lines across pink snow and stone. We bathed in the buttery light, reluctant to descend and declare the day done.

Along the edge of the plateau we met a series of brightly coloured helmet-clad figures. Some sat alone, hunched at the cliff edge like fishermen waiting for a bite. Rope passed through their hands, disappearing down the frozen vertical drop. Others stood in pairs, metal clanking from their waists while they coiled ropes. This was one of my first brushes with climbers. I called hello, grinning like a lunatic, high on the glow of our day, expecting a rhapsodic exchange. I got nothing of the sort.

My greetings were met with short nods and brief smiles. The helmet-wearers seemed cold, distant. A little rude. Why didn't they greet me with the same gusto? Why weren't they surveying the world around them with enraptured wonder like the rest of us? Climbers, I concluded, are a strange, obsessive type, clearly missing out on the wider point of the mountains.

—

The Cairngorms are a strange place to end a book about rock climbing. These mountains, some of the highest in the British Isles, do not form sublime rocky peaks. They are not like the Cuillin, where cliffs and precipices occupy every aspect of the terrain. Nor are they like Ben Nevis or the mountains of Glencoe, north Wales and the Lake District, where the volcanic rock has weathered into defined formations that lead the eye upwards, scaling the steep lines to find the journey towards the top.

The Cairngorms are rounded mountains that can seem topless – or all top. The plateau is the largest tract of high land in Britain. These hills, the weathered roots of ancient mountains, are typically composed of sweeping, curving lines, which makes their forms distinctive and subtle. There is something slightly disorientating about such vast edgelessness. High on the plateau and its surrounding mountains, the slopes meet the sky and fall away in huge curving arcs that mimic the curvature of the Earth. Scale is hard to grasp in such a vast, featureless place.

These hills are better known as a winter sports destination because their elevation and location in the northeast of Scotland gives rise to a particular set of conditions. The Cairngorms act like a giant freezer in the winter. They are sub-arctic, closer in character to Scandinavian landscapes and environments. In this harsh habitat, different species thrive. Up on the hill, you meet northern creatures like the mountain hare and ptarmigan who turn white in the winter, the reindeer who browse the plateau and the snow bunting whose voice fills the frozen corries with a startling lyricism.

When I moved to the Cairngorms in August 2017, this vast, beautiful and intimidating land became part of my everyday life. Every day I looked towards those hills, watching their big blue forms stand clear or vanish inside a thick cloak of cloud. Sometimes they disappeared for days or weeks at a time, eventually emerging, changed. Sometimes they came out wearing the pristine gleam of white snow; sometimes they had been stripped clear.

Work took me north. I started a role for the Cairngorms

National Park Authority, focused on education and inclusion. My job was to help a greater diversity of people engage with the national park, which required a good understanding of the place. In my early weeks, as I chatted with colleagues, the scale of this task soon became apparent. Pinned to the walls of every office were huge maps of the park, showing the 260-mile boundary line, encircling an area of land twice the size of the Lake District. Inside this area lay a huge range of habitats, landforms, communities and environments, from farmland to Scandinavian pine forests to pristine salmon rivers and extensive tracts of grouse moorland. There are whisky distilleries and timber yards, ski resorts and a number of villages composed of squat granite cottages. Each town, from Aviemore to Grantown, Tomintoul, Braemar and Ballater, has its own unique character. A new project began to take shape. I wanted to grasp the whole of the Cairngorms – to understand this place in its entirety.

Just as I had done before in Grasmere, I headed out as much as possible, delving into as many places as I could. I followed rivers, got lost in the forests and stumbled over heather moorland set alive in glorious summer blooms of purple, pink and lilac, watching golden eagles circle overhead. Depending where I went, I might walk all day and meet no one. In these remote spaces, hares became frequent if startling companions.

The straths, glens and lower hills held plenty of interest but the mountaineer in me was always drawn to the plateau, desperate to be up exploring the high lands. There was Ben Macdui and Braeriach, Cairngorm, Sgòr Gaoith and Bynack More – mountains with names and personalities to grasp, each posing a unique challenge. For to reach any of those spots requires a substantial journey into the harsh elemental realm of the Cairngorms. Venturing out onto the plateau alone can be a real joy. On still, clear days, the rolling expanse of boulders, gravels, ice and mosses is heavenly and there are moments where the vast openness catches you unawares and you marvel at the scale of it all. But the plateau can also be frightening and dangerous. The altitude, coupled with our volatile island weather system, means that the good days are the exception, not the rule. Conditions change, fast. The plateau can soon become one of the most challenging environments in the UK, with 100-mile-per-hour winds, blizzards, white-outs, driving rain and sub-arctic temperatures. On a world scale, these mountains are small but what they lack in height, they more than make up for in conditions. Expert mountaineers say that the brutal elements here provide good training for mountaineering around the world.

Navigating through a white-out on the plateau is an extreme physical and mental challenge. Your body is cocooned in layer upon layer of technical clothing, and yet still the freezing wind bites. You pull your hood up, tight, and wear ski-goggles to protect your eyes from the razor-sharp blast of spindrift. A piece of hair escapes from your hat and hood: you cannot remove your thick mittens to tuck it away and so the strand becomes an icicle that lashes against your raw cheeks. Trudging on through the deep snow in those perishing conditions, energy is soon sapped. Calories burn at an extraordinary rate.

You look around, but cannot see anything. Everything is white. The ground and the sky have merged into a brutal, frozen blank. In one mitten, you hold a small plastic plate: a compass, with a critical red arrow. You walk on this bearing, counting your paces, keeping faith in the system – you know what you are doing, but you are still praying. With so few features on that rolling icy expanse, even the experts get it wrong sometimes. Among the many cautionary tales passed around the community, I remember one guide sharing her story of leading a group through a brutal blizzard when the ground suddenly fell beneath her. She had walked off a cornice and plummeted, tumbling down for hundreds of feet into the corrie below. Miraculously, she hit no rocks and survived, unscathed.

The Cairngorms are a difficult place to get to know.

—

Guiding many of these explorations was a book by the Aberdonian hillwalker and writer, Nan Shepherd. I first read *The Living Mountain*, her remarkable book on the Cairngorms, years before, back in my Liverpool days. I remember sitting in the Egg café on some woozy afternoon when cutlery clattered, people chattered and the coffee machine roared furiously, blasting steam into swirling foaming milk; but reading Shepherd's bewitching words, all that noise faded. I was transported.

Her compelling and poetic account of the Cairngorm mountains leaped from the page in vivid detail. Here was a refreshing voice offering delightful new ways of approaching the uplands. Like many other hill folk, she initially made for the summits. But in time she left the peaks behind and began to explore more widely. She wandered into high corries and found hidden lochans and remote springs of water. She watched the birds, plants and animals, observing how they moved and lived within this hostile environment. She attended to the play of elements and light. In her vision, the mountains are multi-layered and all-encompassing. Her meditative study reveals how many parts make up the whole, showing how one might grasp the totality of a mountain.

This was a vital perspective.

As I became more immersed in the world of mountaineering, I often met a certain goal-oriented mindset. Reducing huge landscapes and environments to peaks that must be conquered in good time was common practice. But such an approach sat uneasily with me. It seemed a little arrogant; a little narrow-minded; a little unimaginative. Surely it was missing the point? But then, what was the point? Shepherd's writing helped me to steer another course in the mountains. Returning to her words again and again, I saw how one could go more openly into the hills, taking a wider perspective for a deeper experience. Influenced by Eastern philosophy and Zen Buddhism, Shepherd sought to dissolve the ego and reach a state of oneness with the world.

'To know Being, this is the final grace accorded from the mountain.'[24]

The human body is central to Shepherd's process of being in the Cairngorms and her writing is acutely sensory. Sleeping on Braeriach, rolling in heather, drinking from burns, peering at mountains upside down through her legs; Shepherd teaches how the body can be an instrument that establishes a profound connection between self and mountain. She reveals how the mountain is not just 'out there': the mountain also lies within. Inspired by this approach, when I moved up north I explored the Cairngorms in different seasons and weathers, returning, revisiting and re-treading old paths where I always discovered new things. I brought my focus a little closer. I stopped thinking about distant destinations and started noticing the feel of the ground beneath my feet. The way the wind affected my movement. The temperature of air on skin. Lichen on rocks. I began to find an intimate scale within the vast round hills, and the Cairngorms opened out in spellbinding detail. As Nan Shepherd concludes:

> Knowing another is endless. And I have discovered that man's experience of them enlarges rock, flower and bird. The thing to be known grows with the knowing.[25]

———

At the edge of the plateau, in a granite buttress that towers over Coire an Lochan, two rock faces are severed by a deep cut. The cleft is clear and dark; the line is striking. As I became familiar with the Cairngorm mountain world – growing more comfortable with its vast spaces, changing moods and subtle tones – I was drawn to the rock. I had spent much time on foot and now I wanted to use my hands as well. I wanted to know another aspect of the plateau by uncovering some of the mysteries of the granite. Savage Slit was compelling. The problem became urgent.

This was, in a sense, a goal, and with my desire to climb it well I was perhaps chasing an achievement, violating the ethos that I so admired and respected in Nan Shepherd. But if rock climbing were merely a ticklist exercise of conquest and attainment, I would have long since lost interest in the activity. Completing the route is only part of the story. I was coming to learn that a route is also a process, an excuse, an opening to find another way in. Climbing can be an experiment, an exploration and an investigation – a way of feeling the landscape.

While Nan Shepherd was an inspiring provocation, I was also conscious that, born in 1893, she came to the Cairngorms in a different time and at a very different moment. Mountain culture had moved on since her walking days in the twentieth century. The booming outdoor industry had led to many technical innovations. Gore-Tex, GPS and state-of-the-art climbing equipment now existed. We had accurate mountain weather forecasts and went out armed with mobile phones from which we could call for help – or capture our joys in beaming images to be shared with friends and strangers across global social media platforms. Feminism had progressed. Many women now enjoyed far greater rights and freedoms than ever before, and out in the hills I met increasing numbers of women walking, skiing and climbing. With the mounting pressure of climate change, conservation and environmentalism had a new urgency. The hills were the same, but the landscape around them had changed.

Despite my ambition, there was also something about Savage Slit that made me feel a little uneasy. This was no roadside crag. To reach the climb, I would have to walk uphill for an hour and a half with a heavy bag on my back. After all that work, would I still have the strength to climb? The route sits on a buttress that begins at 1,030 metres above sea level, just shy of the summit of Snowdon. Scale works differently in the Cairngorms. How would the height affect the climb?

I suggested Savage Slit to my friend Anta and, although she had already climbed the route, she immediately agreed to do it again. With a big smile, an infectious laugh and huge enthusiasm, Anta is always up for an adventure. Originally from Latvia, when she discovered mountains she left her flat homeland behind and has never looked back. Working as a ski, snowboard and climbing instructor in the Alps and Cairngorms, she has helped many people from all walks of life to discover a passion for the outdoors. Before moving north, I knew Anta a little. We had both been on the same trip to Kalymnos and traversed the Cuillin together, but it wasn't until we were thrown together by geography that we formed a strong friendship and an entertaining climbing partnership.

On the drive up to the ski car park, Anta reassured me.

'The route is straightforward. You'll lead it no problem.'

She has a good eye for movement on rock. Watching climbers, she will often make perceptive comments about their style. Anta had a high opinion of my climbing – often much higher than my own – but I trusted her judgement and lapped up her encouragement.

We parked the car ready to begin the walk-in when we met our first challenge.

Anta, who had been rummaging through her kit for some time, moaned and looked up with frenzied eyes.

'What's up?'

'I've not got my belay device.'

This is the small metal plate through which you feed the rope while your partner climbs. Should the climber slip, the device enables you to lock the rope off and catch their fall. I had mine; but on a multi-pitch route like Savage Slit we needed one each. We could have made do with an Italian hitch (a more traditional approach using an adjustable knot) but I had never done this before and did not feel confident putting a new skill into practice on a mountain route.

I racked my brains, desperate to get on the rock.

'Shall we drive back to Aviemore? We could grab a belay device from the shops there?'

This would be an hour's round trip: not ideal. Anta had a better suggestion.

'Let's try Glenmore Lodge. If my mate James is working he could lend us his.'

'Yep. Great. Let's do it!'

Thirty minutes later – after a speedy drive and an embarrassing conversation with the young male receptionist ('Ah, the old belay device, you won't be getting far without that!') – we were back in the ski car park, armed with two belay devices, ready to begin again.

I shouldered my bag and we started walking.

Passing through the ski-centre paraphernalia of wires, buildings, paths, cables and fences, I wondered how the day would pan out after this garbled beginning. Was this a sign? The first in a series of mistakes and mishaps? Doubts about our planned undertaking began to creep in. This was no good. Best to climb with a quiet mind. Rather than spend the next hour and a half ruminating over potential problems, I turned my focus elsewhere.

Leaving behind the ski centre, our walk-in to Coire an Lochan took us out across the front of the northern corries. In the Cairngorms, every crag is remote. The closest ones require an hour of strenuous walking; the more remote ones take three or four hours to reach. For some, you have to walk up onto the plateau and then drop back down again, perhaps even clambering over a Munro in the process. Sometimes the distance can be alleviated with a mountain bike, if you are prepared to take on a rough ride up long tracks into the hills with a heavy bag on your back. As well as the climbing gear, ropes, food and layers, you might also carry a sleeping bag, roll mat, tent and stove – if you decide to camp out to gain a couple of days on the rock. There are no shortcuts to climbing in the Cairngorms. You have to be committed.

For many climbers, a long walk-in is seriously off-putting. As climbing becomes increasingly popular, with huge numbers of people embracing the sport through indoor gyms and climbing centres, the outdoors is not seeing the same boom. Fashions change. Today, the mountain crags are often quiet. As a general rule, the further the crag lies from the road, the fewer people you will meet on the rock. For the efficient modern climber, intent upon packing a certain number of routes in at a certain grade, a long walk-in is a waste of time and energy. Why spend three hours slogging uphill with a heavy bag when you could drive to a crag or boulder and leap onto the rock within ten minutes? However, within the rapidly expanding and diversifying community of climbers, there remains a dedicated enclave of tradition-alists who still take on the mountain routes. Many of these find walking boring, but will suffer the approach as a neces-sary means to an end. A few masochists enjoy the march, reframing a failed mission into the mountains as 'training', or the rather more prosaic 'taking the tools for a walk'. There are some climbers though who relish the long immersion of a big approach.

Walking in through those high rolling slopes, we passed

gnarled Scots pines, no higher than my knees, the branches stretched out on one side like the tail of a kite. I love meeting these hardy hill dwarfs. Growing up here, at 800 metres' altitude, they seem so unlikely. Across so much of the British uplands, you rarely encounter trees and yet here – on wind-scoured slopes that are often covered in snow and ice – these little pioneers are creeping up the hillside. The change is small but significant. On this patch of the Cairngorms, there has been a shift in how the land is managed. Sheep do not graze here and deer numbers are kept low. As a result, over the past few decades, the forest edges have softened. Scots pine, birch and rowan are creeping up the hillsides, creating a natural tree line. When I walk with older hill folk, they tell me how significant this is. They tell me how different these hills looked in the 1980s. Their voices wobble when they tell me they never thought they'd see this change happen in their lifetime. A key part of the mountain ecosystem is returning. A greater variety of plants, animals and insects makes the land more resilient. There is strength in diversity.

'What's that?' I stepped off the path, striding across moss, grass and heather to examine a scarlet blob growing inches from the ground. It looked a like a bright red blackberry.

'Cloudberries!' cried Anta in delight, bounding over to join me.

'Cloudberries? What are they? Can you eat them?'

'Of course! They grow in Latvia; I've not seen them here before.'

My fingers pushed through the leaves, reaching for the scarlet specimen.

'Wait – that's not ripe yet.'

There was a whole cluster of these strange fruits, standing

heavy on delicate stems. From red to pink, orange to pale yellow, the berries ranged in shades across the sunset spectrum. Anta placed one in my upturned palm that was yellow-orange.

'Try this one.'

I put the berry in my mouth and bit cautiously. Juice burst onto my tongue. Creamy, sweet like raspberry and sharp like gooseberry: I chewed thoughtfully – the taste was odd – but I knew I wanted another and so we picked and picked, leaving the path to make our own trail uphill.

——

Inside the bowl of Coire an Lochain, the ground fell away. Two ravens detached themselves from a rock tower, flying out, croaking, continuing their conversation while black fingers stretched across the sky. Insects hummed. A light breeze ruffled the surface of the steely-turquoise lochan and a floral scent hung in the air. I like Coire an Lochain. This corrie feels quieter and more forgiving than its neighbour, Coire an t-Sneachda, from which it is separated by the rocky spur of Fiacaill Ridge. In Coire an t-Sneachda, you cannot escape the rock. The walls are sharp and fractured, and below the cliffs granite boulders are strewn right across the basin. That corrie feels restless, forceful and on edge. In Coire an Lochain, the cliffs cluster higher, slightly tucked away, making them slightly more elusive, creating a provocation that draws me in.

One last slog – one final steep, slippery slope to pant and struggle up – and finally we reached the foot of the buttress. Here, I surveyed Savage Slit up close for the first time. The route was first climbed in 1945 by a couple of lads from Inverness, Richard Frere and Kenneth Robertson. Since their ascent, the route has become a much-loved classic. I could see why. The line was even more compelling than I had imagined. Two clean rock faces stretched up towards the blue sky. With distinctive architecture, the granite was fractured into blocks of titanic masonry. Between these faces was the slit: straight, black and unequivocal. You could drop a rope from the top and it would hardly take a more direct line to the foot of the crag.

I quickly dug out my climbing kit, eager to get on rock, but Anta was in less of a flurry. She took her time and once she was ready, she led the first pitch, climbing through ten metres of broken rock and ramps to the reach foot of the slit. We had agreed that I would lead the upper pitches.

She belayed me up and I took over. From below, I had thought I would climb inside the slit, finding handholds and foot placements within the dark column. Yet when I got there, I discovered the opening was too wide: the slit was a loose sock; it would not hug my body. I looked out to the rock face and considered the blocks there. They were defined and regular, offering plenty of pockets for hands and feet, but each block was rounded. There were no sharp edges to hang off; nothing to pinch. Instead, I had to curve my hands around the blocks, trusting the contact between skin and stone. The curves of the plateau are mirrored in its stones. I placed my right hand onto a sloping edge, found another curved lip for my right foot and tentatively stepped up, pulling my palm into the granite. My hand held and my toes stayed on. The granite was smooth and grainy: the crystals gripped without scratching my skin. My confidence grew and I pushed against the stone, trusting the friction. The movement felt good.

My interest in the granite did not begin with the cliffs. Roaming the plateau on foot, I became captivated by the smaller formations. On certain peaks, forms emerged through the mist, rising clear and defined, solid and intriguing, weathered into the most appealing rounded shapes. They were tors: little blocky outcrops that had survived the scraping of the Ice Ages to continue standing free on the plateau. The Barns of Bynack are particularly striking. Circling this rocky mass one afternoon, I was mesmerised by the shapes, colours and textures. From every angle, the granite seemed different. At a distance, the tors cluster in a series of upright bodies like whales breaching the sea. Up close, the rough skin and wrinkles reminded me of the flank of an elephant. My hands roamed across the curved edges, pulling the granite into my palms to see how it felt. The surface was grainy, full of crystals. Some were large and sharp and others were small and soft. The grip was impeccable. From some angles, the surfaces wore a bleached shade of uniform grey; then again, tilt your head, move in closer, find another light and vivid colours shine through. The granite is pink, grey, white, luminous green, soft blue and black, for as well as the stone crystals, the surface is also clothed in lichens and mosses. There was something here that held me captive. Somewhere within these forms lay the substance of the Cairngorms.

Cairngorm granite has a violent origin story. It was fired into existence during the Caledonian orogeny some 427 million years ago. Continents collided, the Iapetus Ocean closed and rock was folded, crumpled, cooked and uplifted.

From the upheaval, an immense chain of mountain peaks the size of the Himalayas rose up. The remnants can still be found stretching from Norway, through Scotland into Ireland, Greenland and America. During all of this activity, batholiths of molten rock intruded into spaces deep underground, cooling slowly below the Earth's crust. Crystals of grey quartz, pink and white feldspar, and flakes of black biotite mica formed, along with a rarer smoky-quartz known as a cairngorm. During the nineteenth century, people took to the plateau armed with shovels, digging holes and prising stones in pursuit of this treasured gemstone.

———

On Savage Slit, I clambered up the ledges, sticking to the surface matter. Ivory scratches appeared on the pink-grey face, showing the passage of axe and crampon. The route has become a popular winter climb and I wondered what stories lay around these marks. How many epics, tragedies and glowing ecstasies had come to pass on these same rocks?

Navigating the summer stone with ease, I enjoyed the elastic stretch of bridging across the slit and rebounding between the sides. The climbing was smooth, the route was clear, my gear was spaced, but I felt well protected. This was not how I had imagined Savage Slit. I had expected drama and tension; to meet a great challenge; to feel my nerves singing with the mountain exposure. Instead, I felt comfortable. Like a warm river on a hot afternoon, the rock welcomed my body.

Ahead, however, the flow was broken. The slit was plugged by a huge chockstone. Ice and water must have worked at it, slowly fracturing and loosening the roots, until the connection between block and rock face was finally severed. Instead of crashing down to the corrie below, the block had simply slumped into the slit, where it wedged fast. I contemplated my approach to this obstacle. When Frere climbed Savage Slit, at this point he headed inside the slit. For him, an early climber on the first ascent of the route, squirming inside the grimy darkness was safer than tackling the exposed face. Seventy years later, climbing has changed. There was no way that I was going to writhe around in the dark. I tackled the chockstone direct, reaching my arms to the back of the block and plunging my feet into cracks before walking them up the stone as I hauled my body up and over. My muscles fired up, my heart thumped, and I stood on top, grinning.

From this wide stance, I peered down into the slit and my stomach flipped. I was not used to openings like this. On long multi-pitch mountain routes, I had grown accustomed to the feeling of space below my feet and the glimpses of vast panoramas at my side, but here, before me, where rock should meet my gaze, there was a void. The slit ran deep into the mountain, stretching back and back. There was something peculiarly awful about it. I pushed my shoulders further in for a better view. My eyes slowly adjusted to the gloom. Far below, in the murky depths of the cleft, lay scattered debris from past climbers. A water bottle. A harness. A shoe.

'Anna! Is that your shoe?'

Anta was manically gesturing into the slit.

I peered down into the abyss again. There, in among the dust and dirt at the foot of the tomb, was the shoe. A green and black approach shoe: identical to the ones I had walked in with. Oh God – was it mine? Heart pounding, I seized my rucksack and pummelled the fabric, feeling for my shoes. Hands located first one, then the other. Thank God.

'No! It's OK! I've got both of mine.'

'Ha! I bet that dude had a hard time walking out with just one shoe!'

On the final section of the climb, as we drew nearer to the sky, the slit widened and I chimneyed, pressing my back against the cool wall, moving my feet up the other side, gradually working my torso up the gap. The movement was awkward but the slit felt comfortable. The granite held me tight. This really was a beautiful line.

Then, all too soon, the line gave way to broken rock and grassy ramps. The climb was over. Setting up the final anchors, I felt the slightest twinge of disappointment. I had loved the situation, the route, the rock, and I wanted more. Eighty metres was not enough. Or perhaps the climb wasn't quite challenging enough. Having built Savage Slit up in my head, I had considered it a great climbing test piece; my first proper route high in the Cairngorms. I thought the exposure and situation might frighten me – but I had actually found the climb pretty straightforward. Easy, even.

I had moved on as a climber. I was no longer starting at sea level, meeting the rock within the blinding haze of inexperience. The lofty situation did not terrify me as that atmospheric route on Great Gable had once done. Over the years, I had grown comfortable moving on rock and now I longed to do more of it, taking on more intricate and demanding routes into the mountains.

Settling into the rhythm of belaying, I relaxed and looked

out across the strath. Micro-rock focus gave way to expanded vision. I remembered where we were – on the Cairngorm plateau, standing higher than any peak in England or Wales. Far below were wind turbines and tiny towns; forests, lochs and distant mountains. To the north, a tender blue streak marked the Moray Firth. Sometimes, the Cairngorms are generous. That afternoon, the plateau was remarkably peaceful. Grass heads fluttered and the quartz gravel beds shone like waves blown onto the sea. We packed away our gear and let gravity carry us back out.

———

If climbing in the Cairngorms starts to feel a little too sublime and esoteric – you begin to feel a touch too light, radiating the giddy spirit that Nan Shepherd calls *fey* – Aviemore can always be relied upon to bring you back down with a bump. Rounding off our day on Savage Slit, we stopped in town to follow up on a recommendation from a fellow mountaineer. He reckoned there was a chip shop there which served up a first-rate version of a unique Scottish delicacy. I had not tried deep-fried pizza before, but that evening, after a good day on the hill, the appetite was there. We got in the queue.

It moved slowly.

Our hunger grew – our stomachs growling and protesting – minds listless and irritable.

Patience.

Order placed, we took a number, trying to wait nonchalantly.

Time was moving slowly.

But then the moment came. Two half-moon pasties emerged gleaming from the fryer.

We raced forwards and took the treats back to our table where we crunched through the crispy batter with relish, releasing a gooey mess of cheese, tomato and dough, all of which oozed together in delicious salty greasy mouthfuls.

The verdict: much better than expected. The aftermath: it seemed as though someone had put a stone in my stomach.

———

Rock climbing in the Cairngorms was slower to develop than in other parts of the UK. The earliest activity centred on Lochnagar, the great romantic mountain of Royal Deeside. Lord Byron introduced the mountain to the national imagination in 1807 with his poem 'Lachin y Gair', or 'Dark Lochnagar', and the mountain's fame was fixed when Queen Victoria bought the Balmoral Estate in the 1840s. The queen herself climbed to the summit in 1848 with the help of ponies (as was common practice then). Around this time, the mountain's name was changed to Lochnagar, meaning 'small loch of noise'. The original Gaelic name is Beinn nan Ciochan, the hill of the breasts, and the two peaks on the summit ridge are Cac Carn Beag and Cac Carn Mor: 'little shit cairn' and 'big shit cairn'. Such names clearly did not provide the right footing for the sublime pinnacle of the Romantic Highlands.

The climbers came in the 1890s, when pioneers began to break away from the main path to the summit, seeking new lines on the steep corrie walls. These early routes took to the gullies – water-worn ravines and channels that open between clean rock faces – spaces where Victorian climbers, with limited equipment, felt safer. However, gully climbing does not provide the most inspiring route up a mountain. Tom Patey, a talented climber, writer and doctor who cut his teeth on Cairngorms rock when studying at Aberdeen University, faithfully captures the particular quality of these mountain ducts in an essay for the *Scottish Mountaineering Club Journal*:

> Most gullies are unpleasant. A Cairngorm gully is doubly so. It is the sort of place you would incarcerate your worst enemy; a dank gloomy prison where moisture seeps from every fissure and 'all the air a solemn stillness holds' – save for a constant drip, drip from many a greasy moss-enshrouded chockstone and the occasional dull thud as another ledge sloughs away in a welter of slime and rubble.
>
> The early mountaineers, who revelled in the false security of gullies and chimneys and spurned the hazardous freedom of the open face, must have found the Cairngorms a vertical Mecca. Here were any number of holdless muddy walls against which to erect a pyramid of stout fellows in tweed jackets, greasy constricted chimneys where they might squirm and wriggle to the hearts' content [. . .].[26]

Those early gully routes on Lochnagar, with all their dripping, greasy slime and loose rock, are rarely climbed now, but when the snow comes in, briefly burying all that unpleasant matter beneath a thick white veneer, they become cherished winter routes.

Such repugnant summer routes gave rise to the belief that Cairngorms rock was poor quality – although the more optimistic climbers still found some merit in sticking to those difficult lines.[27] Jim Bell, a leading Scottish mountaineer, famously claimed: 'Any fool can climb good rock but it takes craft and cunning to get up vegetatious schist and granite.' His partner Bill Murray agreed, explaining that they were bound for Lochnagar, 'the greatest citadel of vegetatious granite'.[28] Things changed when climbers left the gullies and ventured out onto the open granite faces. This movement was primarily led by a dedicated crew of Aberdonians who cycled or caught the bus to Braemar to spend the weekend in the hills; although, as better lines were found, more climbers came in from other parts to try the granite for themselves. Moving beyond Lochnagar, the adventurous pioneers headed further into the massif. Below the peaks of Ben Macdui, Beinn a' Bhùird, Braeraich, Sgòr Gaoith and Carn Etchachan, many new routes were uncovered in a surge of activity from the 1940s through to the 1960s. This must have been an exciting time to be a climber in northeast Scotland. Photographs capture groups on hillsides and outside bothies wearing sturdy leather boots, lumpy stockings and woollen jumpers. Ropes are coiled across the body. Cigarettes and pipes sometimes rest in their hands. The climbers look hardy, but rarely serious. They are mostly relaxed and smiling, leaning against rocks, arms wrapped around their companions' shoulders. Among the many men, occasional women appear, such as Nancy Forsyth, a teacher, who led pitches on many first ascents, including the first major rock climb on the Dubh Loch: a 900-foot wander through ribs, grooves and walls named the Labyrinth.[29]

While that era of intensive exploratory climbing has passed, going out to climb in the Cairngorms still feels like

a voyage into the unknown. We prepare by checking forecasts, trying to build a picture of what conditions we will
find on our chosen chunk of granite. But you can rarely be
certain until you get there. The rock might be dry; it might
be wet. Our changeable mountain weather could throw
anything at us. Walking in for hours, crossing crystal-clear
burns, tramping through boulder fields, passing corries and
yellow-green summer hillsides, bound for some remote slab
of granite, I begin to wonder whether the cliff will ever
appear. Within such big, round, rolling features, a sharp rock
line starts to seem highly unlikely. But then I turn a corner,
skirt a steep, grassy terrace or drop down from the plateau,
and a towering granite form appears. Ravens bark, but there
is no one else around. Just you and your partner, immersed
in a world of weathered rock, lichens, the sound of distant
water and ever-changing light. A peregrine circles overhead.
The timelessness of the most distant corries is haunting.

———

On a Saturday in early July, I headed into the Loch Avon
basin to climb on Hell's Lum. The sky was clear and the sun
was splitting the stones. This was during the drought of 2018.
There had been no rain for months. Wildfires raged over
tinder-dry peatbogs, fields, gorse thickets and forests. Across
the Cairngorms, farmers and crofters were struggling. With
so little water around, grass and crops grew slowly; some
perished. To keep the livestock going they turned to deep
water sources, drawing on seldom-used wells and reservoirs,
hoping they wouldn't run dry.

While day after day of cloud-free skies created difficult

conditions for many, some rejoiced. When the sunshine first arrived in early May, climbers headed out and were astonished at what they found. Everything was bone dry. Even the highest, wettest mountain crags. Routes that normally seeped and oozed water had completely dried out. Climbers descending, tired and dehydrated, from the east buttress of Scafell reported in disbelief that there was not a wet hold in Cumbria. We expected rain to come and spoil our fun but it never did. For a few months, we glimpsed what it might be like to be a climber in Spain. With no need to consult weather forecasts or agonise over conditions when planning a day on the rock, anything was possible. Ben and I set out for the pink water-streaked slabs of Hell's Lum to climb the crag classic, the Clean Sweep.

This time, walking in from the ski car park, sun lotion dripped from hot foreheads and we stopped to fill our bottles in the burns, drinking thirstily. The mountain waters were quiet; a gentle murmur rolling down through a hillside shimmering with heat. Inside Coire Domhain, a blackened patch of moss and lichen showed where a snow bed had recently melted.

Tumbling down the rocky path beside the burn that drops into the Loch Avon basin, we chattered to another pair of climbers, also exclaiming on the exceptional conditions. They were heading to the black bastion of Shelterstone crag, an imposing wedge of northeast-facing granite, loaded with extreme routes. Already, a few specks of colour had appeared on that mighty rock face. Like moths to a flame, climbers were drawn out onto the long, high routes. The Scottish mountain crags, which sometimes feel exceptionally quiet and lonely, were buzzing.

We broke away from the main path, hopping across the

burn, traversing steep terraces full of grasses and flowers to reach the foot of Hell's Lum. Here, we met another pair of climbers gearing up at the foot of the Clean Sweep. My heart sank. We could wait and follow them up but the pace would be off. Hovering on pitches, waiting for strangers, does not make for inspiring climbing. The dance would be interrupted. We needed an alternative.

Ben checked the guidebook and made a suggestion.

'What about Salamander? HVS 5a. Six pitches.'

This was harder than the Clean Sweep and considerably more difficult than Savage Slit. Doubts set in. Would I be able to climb it?

That summer I had become comfortable leading that grade on the Moray Firth, but those were short routes on gently featured sandstone. This was 155 metres of granite: a rock that still felt unfamiliar. I had not yet grasped how it worked and was not confident in my ability to move around its strange features and grainy textures. Transferring knowledge from one rock to another is not always straightforward, and sandstone and granite seemed worlds apart.

I took the book and examined the route, checking the line against the rock. Unlike Savage Slit, there was no clearly defined feature to follow. Salamander would take us into a sea of granite slabs, walls and overlaps – a precipice of unknowns to meet and somehow navigate.

Facing swirling doubts, I decided a quick resolution was best.

'Fuck it. Let's do it.'

'It should be fine,' Ben reassured me as we flaked the ropes. 'The third pitch is the crux, so I'll lead first and you can take the easier ones.'

We tied in and Ben started up a flared crack in the shining slab. He moved slowly, tuning into the rock, pausing to jangle through gear, fiddling pieces in.

'Bit of a steep start!'

I watched him closely, twitching the rope through my belay device – now giving slack, now taking in – impatient and nervous. Time crawled.

The pitch was long and Ben was not sure where it ended. Reaching some big ledges, he settled on a stance and I fastened my shoes. With a quick glance to check we had left nothing behind, I sprang onto the granite, ready to stretch my limbs and enter the rock.

I saw why he had hesitated. There were few positive holds on the smooth slab. Perhaps the clue was in the name. Moving like a lizard, I tried an adhesive crawl, connecting palms and feet to the stone. The granite glaze was warm. Hell's Lum is south-facing and the rock was lapping up the sunshine. My palms soaked in this heat, soon growing clammy. Chalk helped: I dipped my hands into the pouch on the back of my harness, smeared my feet and began to trust the excellent grip of granite. It was delicate and bold.

Muscles came to life and as I stretched and reached, I began to feel the flow of energy between body and rock, falling into the rhythm of movement.

At Ben's ledge, I secured myself to the anchor and we began the gear swap: stripping his harness to clip everything onto my own. The next pitch was mine.

Before I could proceed though, we hit a snag.

'Pass us the guidebook,' Ben said. 'I think I've climbed the second pitch too.'

Route-finding can be tricky, especially on long, winding

traditional mountain climbs. Without a line of bolts marking the way or an obvious feature to follow, you must find the line yourself and this can prove surprisingly difficult. A line that seems clear from a distance can vanish once you enter the labyrinth of rock.

'Pitch two: follow easier rocks to a glacis. Pitch three: climb twin cracks up steep slabs left of an obvious corner to a platform.'

We examined the features around us.

Ahead, a pair of cracks ran up the wall. We were near pitch three: Ben had inadvertently climbed a good chunk of pitch two.

It was my turn at the sharp end of the rope and I was now facing the crux pitch.

I paused. Could I lead it? On the Moray sea cliffs I was comfortable on this grade: I had entered a calm and focused space; never panicking, never falling. But this was different. It was on the side of a mountain – already so much higher off the ground than I had ever climbed in Moray. And this was granite. It didn't have the same system of pockets and cracks that lined the sandstone – this rock was subtle, technical and full of improbable moves.

Sensing my hesitation, Ben offered to help: 'Are you happy leading? I'll do it if you want.'

I exhaled and examined the rock ahead. Forget sandstone, forget the drama, forget the setting. I had enjoyed the climbing below and had climbed harder things elsewhere. This was no different. (Just a little higher, a little more exposed, a little more demanding.)

'It's OK. I'll lead.'

I took a final check, rattling through the metal on my

waist and tightening my harness, which dragged heavy on my hips. We had combined racks, which meant I was carrying more weight than usual.

'Ready?'

'Yep.'

'OK. On belay.'

I unclipped from the anchor and stepped up, leaving Ben and the ledge behind.

The slabs rose like waves before me. Ramps curved forwards into scoops that steepened into vertical crests with small overlaps breaking into the next ramp. This was not like Savage Slit, where the rock face is fractured into regular lines and blocks, where my hands and feet could rest securely, with gear readily available. This was delicate. I padded up the slabs, palms on the hot rock, hunting for features. My fingers found whispers in the surface: a crease, a dimple, a blemish. My feet smeared the granite, friction fusing rubber to rock. Mind, muscle and motion: I poured myself into the rock and my body sang with the stone.

The pitch rose. I was reaching the edge of my vocal range.

I needed to get some gear in.

My hope lay in the twin cracks. I stopped in a scoop, intent on finding something. Ahead, the rock steepened. I couldn't climb on without putting some metal in, but this was hardly a comfortable place to stop. There was nothing big enough for me to wrap a hand around. I couldn't lock an arm off and let my weight hang. I gripped one tenuous hold and then another, swapping and changing. This did not feel great. But it seemed the best I could hope for.

Concentrate: place some gear.

I slid a nut into a crack but it didn't sit right. The crack flared, the nut wobbled, I tugged and it popped out.

I tried again with a different-sized piece.

Same problem.

My cheeks flushed and palms prickled. The pressure was mounting. I was far above my last piece of gear and the longer I stood here, the more tired I would become. It would be a serious down-climb or a big fall if I messed this up. I swore. A lot. Ben shouted encouragement.

Keep cool. If I panicked, a tricky situation would soon become desperate.

There must be something here.

Lactic acid burned in my calves. I lifted one leg and shook it out; did the same with the other and then surveyed the openings in the rock again. From Ben's set of tiny brass nuts, I slipped one into a hairline crack. It was paltry, but it held. I looked at a wider slot. Perhaps a cam would fit in there. I pushed one in. It moved around – as cams do – but when I tugged it stayed in place. The pressure eased. I had found protection.

Falling back into the rock, I climbing on through the granite, drinking in the opportunities as they appeared. Here was a finger pinch, now a side pull, there a smear. In a few short, steep moves I was past the crux. The angle eased. I padded up the slabs, my body flowing with comfort and agility. Tension eased and I began to appreciate the rock. This was a great pitch.

At a platform, I found a couple of easy anchors, secured myself and sat cross-legged, peering over the edge.

'Safe, Ben!'

From far below, the call came.

'Off belay!'

I hauled up the ropes, heaping them into a lurid pile of yellow and pink spaghetti beside me. This big table-top surface made a gorgeous belay ledge. There was plenty of room to get comfortable. My shoes, which had been melting to my feet in the hot sun, came off, and I relaxed into the steady pull of belaying. Now halfway up the wall, I surveyed the Loch Avon basin like an eagle from its eyrie.

Gouged out by glaciers, cliffs circle the head of the basin, forming an amphitheatre of rock and water. After heavy rain, the space thunders. Burns plummet down from the plateau in sharp white lines that crash, tumble and roar into the immense loch below. Three miles long, the loch plunges to an astonishing depth of thirty metres, forming a vast repository of crystal-clear Cairngorm water. In winter, the surface freezes over and people ski across it. In summer, the water hits your skin like ice and fire. Plunging in, your chest instantly tightens and the cold creeps into your spine, heading up through the neck to grasp your head with its deep chill.

At the head of the loch was Shelterstone, the cliff that takes its name from a huge boulder perched upon rocks among the rough debris beneath the cliff. The entrance to this primitive shelter does not look much, but squeeze through the tight dark passageway between the rocks and you will emerge into a hidden room beneath the boulder. It is a strange place to sleep. Some fear the crushing claustrophobia and have a restless night below the perched boulder; but in heavy rain the shelter can be most welcome. In the dead of night, when all torches are off and candles extinguished, the darkness is absolute. Drifting in and out of consciousness within that crude interior, the sleeper can feel at once lost and held, as though they are resting inside the belly of a great whale.

Leaving the sunlit boulder, I squinted up at the dark pillars above, trying to find the climbers we had spoken to earlier. They were on Steeple: a long, serious line that lies between the Needle and Haystack. In among the shadowed rock I spotted some colour. A white helmet and a red T-shirt. Below: an orange helmet and a green T-shirt. There they were, a few pitches in. They had asked whether I had ever climbed on Shelterstone and I had laughed the idea off: such extreme granite lines seemed well beyond my ability. But now, sat in the sunshine halfway up Hell's Lum, I began to feel a tickle of intrigue. Perhaps I could, after all, climb on there. Even more surprisingly, perhaps I actually wanted to. Climbing on these big walls was another way to spend time in a remarkable place. Up here, the climbing body could absorb the environment, seeing it from many different aspects.

Beyond the big landscape features, the Loch Avon basin is also striking at a smaller, more intimate scale. I love roaming among the moraines and boulders strewn across the ground between the loch and the cliffs. Down there, during spring, summer and the brief autumn season that passes so soon into winter, astonishing colours and textures nestle between the rocks. From damp, dark nooks, green feathery fern fronds spring up. Harebells, also known as the Scottish bluebell, wave their alluring little flower-caps over tiny yellow roses of tormentil. Purple heather flowers among yellow, green and orange grasses. There are blaeberries, but also another type of blaeberry, with blue leaves and larger fruit – the northern bilberry. Tiny trees are also appearing. Junipers sprawl octopus-like tendrils across boulders, clinging low for shelter. Delicate rowan stems thrust up and occasional small pines hint at the progressive march of the Caledonian forest.

The verdant nature of the lofty Loch Avon basin resembles slopes on the Lofoten Islands in Arctic Norway, another granite region where mosses, flowers, plants and shrubs grow in rich abundance right up the cool, damp hillsides. When I visited that northern land, I was shocked. I never knew a mountain could look like that. Having grown up with the over-grazed British uplands, I had never known anything different. Coming back to the hills of home was depressing. But in the Loch Avon basin, where the land is owned by the RSPB and deer numbers are kept low, I find a glimpse of what our uplands could become. High within our vast remote mountains, wild gardens are growing.

'Right – where we off to next?' Ben's smiling face appeared beside me before he climbed past me to take on the fourth pitch.

We were in the flow now.

The granite sea fragmented. The slabs, bulges and scoops became more irregular, breaking apart. Cracks opened up, offering space for gear. We passed an overlap, moving comfortably through a short dark corner – pushing and pulling, reaching and padding. More slabs came and then a shallow groove. The rock held us and we kept moving, lapping up the granite, the line, the drama and sunshine.

On my lead, I approached a bulging wall of rock: a headwall of huge blocks that cast black shadows. The direct line looked impossible.

But there was another way. Cutting through the blocks there was a chimney slit: just wide enough for a human.

I clambered up, my hands passing over crispy black flakes strewn across the granite slabs. In normal conditions, this would be a viscous slime and my fingers and feet would struggle for purchase, slipping and sliding on the damp matter, growing cold and wet. In rain, these slabs sheen, the whole surface of the cliff set in motion as water slews off.

But on that day, Hell's Lum was exceptionally dry.

At my touch, the black slime crumbled.

Inside the chimney lay the first hint of water on that entire sun-baked rock face. At the back of the shadowed slit, streaks glistened in the darkness, the water shining with its own life. I couldn't remember when it had last rained and so it seemed, in this lofty interior, I had met a secret wellspring of the plateau, a place where liquid bled out from the deepest bowels of the old batholith.

The climbing steepened. I reached into the back of the chimney, finding holds hidden in the cool green enclave. The slit narrowed and the movement changed. Balance and poise shifted into thuggy thrutching. Back against one wall: feet pushed up the other. The wedge was snug and it tightened at the top.

I squeezed through, my hips struggling with the opening. All of the metal gear clipped to my harness made my hips wide, heavy and awkward. I twisted and jiggled and tugged, eventually breaking free.

Ben had a harder time. Following me up with a rucksack on his back, the gap proved awkward. He swore and struggled – I laughed – but he soon got his revenge.

On the final pitch, the rock petered out, breaking into an

open funnel littered with loose rock. Inside the passage sat a huge chockstone, wedged in tight with a tiny gap underneath. As I approached this stone I heard a chuckle and realised what he had done. The ropes did not lead me up the easy line over the top of the stone. The coloured lines disappeared underneath the rock: Ben had squeezed through the tiny gap, which meant that I also had to follow his line. And this time I was carrying the rucksack.

I cursed him. Loudly.

More chuckles came rattling down the gully.

—

With any visit into the Cairngorms, the living moment can be striking. Light changes; new weathers blow in; temperature fluctuates; seasons soon pass. The massif is a vast space that opens and closes: inviting one moment, repelling the next.

Granite gave me another way into this most particular and subtle world. Savage Slit and Salamander provided focal points. On those routes, skin met stone; mind melded with matter and I poured myself into the long lines leading into and out of the weathered bedrock; the substance of the Cairngorms.

Lost in a sea of granite, I was always conscious of my fleshy vulnerability, but within the fluctuations of the rock, I began to find different forms, within myself, to move around that matter. Balance and poise. Rhythm and sequence. Focus, force and supple sensitivity. Creative muscular abilities emerged and through rock climbing – an intense and intimate approach to landscape – I began to grasp something.

Clinging to the pink-grey granite and the fundamental crystals that had formed aeons ago, deep within the Earth, at moments, I had a sense of how different scales of life and time – the vast and the minute, the ancient and the present – can coexist at certain points, quite comfortably. The feeling was fleeting, passing all too quickly, leaving me once again with a sense of inadequacy. I hadn't quite grasped it. There was more to be done.

Epilogue

CREAG AN DUBH LOCH

GRANITE

September 2020. The air smells different – slightly sharp, with the first hint of dank decay. Mushrooms bloom after rain and the weeping tresses of the birch trees are starting to turn golden. Suddenly the days feel much shorter. Summer is coming to a close.

Then a spell of fine weather comes in. The mornings start cool, with a misty haze that soon burns off, leaving the hills and glens basking in bright September sunshine. Across Aberdeenshire, farmers race out with tractors and combines, rushing to complete the harvest before the long winter sets in. Like the farmers, we anxiously watch the sky and check forecasts, hoping that this spell will last. Praying for one more good day for one last trip to the Dubh Loch.

That day arrives. Monday morning and we're up at six for a wordless breakfast.

The sky lightens on the drive to Glen Muick and we see that conditions have changed. The blue skies have gone. A vast cloudscape has flooded in from the southwest, filling the high atmosphere with flowing bubbles and waves of vapour. The sun rises, turning a clutch of eastern clouds rosy-golden. On the ground, trees and grasses lurch and writhe under blasts of powerful wind. The weather is turning.

I'm slightly nervous. I've wanted to climb on the Dubh Loch for a while now. At a kilometre long and 300 metres high, it is one of the biggest mountain cliffs in the UK, and yet – tucked away in a far-flung corner of the Cairngorms – few have heard of it. Those who have climbed on the Dubh Loch talk of technical granite, tricky route-finding and committing lines. It is not the cliff for a beginner. For some, this distant and enigmatic hunk of granite becomes a deep-rooted obsession.

On my first visit to the Dubh Loch, despite the immense stature of the cliff, I did not see the rock until I was stood metres away, straining my neck to look up into its dark precipices. That was a deathly still August day. We cycled then hid the bikes at the end of Loch Muick and tramped uphill, following a small gravel path winding through purple flowering heather, entering thick, damp cloud. Sounds were muffled. Boulders loomed beside the path like lurking watchmen. We could have been on any path into any mountain. I had no sense of where we were.

The fog thickened. The path petered out and we hopped along a boggy trail. Through the mist a surface emerged like a mirage: smooth and light; shining and melding into the fog. We had reached the loch. Inside this deep hollow, scoured from the plateau by ice and water, there are two immense landscape features – both known as the Dubh Loch. One is a large black lake with golden granite sands. The other is Creag an Dubh Loch: the crag of the black loch. In this long-standing partnership, the crag has taken the name of the loch.

We walked on and still the cliff was hidden. At the head of the loch, in the thick morning fog, it was hard to tell where the water ended and the cloud began. We met a burn pouring with water from the plateau. The stepping stones were submerged. I took my shoes off and waded across, stumbling on the sharp, slippery edges that lay beneath the flow. Still the cliff was hidden.

We slogged uphill, clambering through wet heather, moss and blaeberry bushes, pausing to catch breath, tongues turning purple from ripe fruit. The boulders grew bigger, more frequent, looser. I panted and sweated, now focusing on careful footwork, hopping from one rocking stone to another. And then, through the fog, a towering wall of corners, hanging blocks and smooth slabs appeared. There were shining charcoal-grey walls, dark roofs, blunt arêtes and black, glistening cracks. The Dubh Loch had materialised. This was one of the finest and most intimidating walls I had ever seen.

Ropes, harness, gear and helmets came out. We picked our line and tried to climb but conditions were treacherous. Water seeped and streaked down the slabs. One wrong foot and a huge pendulous fall would follow. The Dubh Loch must have been caught in a localised thunderstorm: a midsummer cloudburst had drenched everything.

Standing inside those steep gully walls, we soon learned that water was not the only issue. Rising from the ground, swarming in the still air, came thick black clouds of hungry midges. The tiny insects crawled across skin and clothes, flying into eyes, ears, mouths and noses, biting anything that was exposed. We flapped and waved; tried repellent and head nets, but the numbers were extraordinary.

Midges – the scourge of many a peaceful summer hour in the hills – thrive in warm, damp conditions. The peatbogs and wet grasslands across the British Isles provide the perfect nursing ground for these horrors. It is said that the midge can fly no faster than three miles per hour – so a walker can generally outpace them. But pause for a moment on a still summer day and you will soon notice a few grey smudges hovering in your vision. As you linger on that spot to catch your breath and admire the view, perhaps taking a swig from your water bottle and reaching for your camera, the vampires will crowd in, soon massing into a hungry biting swarm. Camping is hell. And climbing, which involves much time standing on belay ledges and slow movements up the rock face, becomes horrific.

Desperate to escape the onslaught, we admitted defeat, stuffing away the ropes and gear with none of the usual care, and ran, choking, coughing and cursing back down to seek respite in the loch.

Melting into the rippling black depths, skin and limbs relaxed and I rolled in the waters, pushing out further towards the middle, where I stopped, buoyed, bobbing to gaze back up towards the cliff face. During all of that heated kerfuffle, the cloud had lifted and the Dubh Loch had emerged. An intricate mass of granite walls, slabs and lines stretched up for hundreds of metres towards the plateau high above. I had to return.

———

As we march up that same long walk-in from Loch Muick, things feel different. The burns are quiet and easy to cross; the clouds are sat much higher. But the air is restless. Powerful gusts snatch at my hair and breath, pushing me back down the path, throwing me off balance.

I push back.

Dan, my partner for the day, heralds the blast a 'good drying wind', adding it to the tally of positive omens for our day on the Dubh Loch.

Just a few days ago, he was up here with another friend on a route called the Kraken. Their day started well. The first section of rock looked dry and so the Dubh Loch lured the eager climbers in. Gradually, as they moved up the long line, things changed. Their route from the foot of the gully to the top of the plateau morphed into something of an epic.

Higher up the wall, they discovered that everything was sopping wet. They moved slowly, taking care not to slip on the wet rock and moss. Ninety metres in – halfway – they met the grass moustache: a ledge of thick mosses, grasses and blaeberries; hands plunged deep into the greenery at the back of the moustache, feet edged across the rock below in the most peculiar traverse. Fingers grew numb and a deep chill set in from handling all that damp matter. Nonetheless, they climbed on, leading up through pitch after pitch in conditions that they later reported felt more like winter than summer climbing. This was mid-September. Night crept up on them. They topped out in the dark, armed with only one head torch. The descent and long walk-out took on a night-mare quality. Finally, at 2.27 a.m., my phone lit up with the safe-and-well message:

'Just got back. Had an adventure.'

With this fresh tale of mishap, I approach the Dubh Loch with a renewed sense of caution. This time we start earlier and ensure we both have a head torch. But in taking on a long mountain route, there is always a degree of unpredict-ability. Such uncertainty is part of the magic.

We stop at the head of the loch. It is cold in the wind so we pile on layers and examine the rock from a distance. Occasional dark seep lines run down from the blackest roofs, but for the most part, the Dubh Loch wears the dull-grey gleam of dry rock. Excitement flickers. Perhaps we will have a good day after all. Perhaps at this time of year, at this end of the season, something special will happen. Perhaps we are out on the last day of the Scottish summer mountain season.

Fighting the wind, we bring out the route guide. The photocopied sheets flap like a trapped bird, frantic to be freed. We pin down the corners, looking for Cayman, a ten-pitch E2 that runs up from the foot of a buttress, weaving and climbing through the granite face towards the plateau high above.

———

At the foot of the buttress, we prepare for the climb. Bags are dropped and out come harnesses, ropes, gear, helmets, chalk and climbing shoes. I put on a jumper, zip my coat and stuff some chocolate bars into my trainers, which I clip to the back of my harness. We will travel light up the wall: no rucksack, no spare layers, no water.

The horizon has shifted. Up close, the immense rock face has grown in stature. The upper reaches have vanished behind the more immediate bulges, overlaps, breaks and contortions. The detail starts to press in, but until I get on the rock, I have little idea what to expect. I've been told that the climbing on the Dubh Loch is unlike anything else.

Jules Lines, a quiet legend of Cairngorms climbing, who has put in many hours on this face, offers a good insight into the peculiar nature of this rock:

There's a real art to climbing on the Dubh Loch – indeed the climbing is unique, and subtleties of improvisation in body tension and balance are required to tackle these formidable overlaps, blank grooves and smooth arêtes. Holds are sparse, but uncannily there are always enough to just get by. Honed strong men with rubber tendons and pliers for fingers aren't going to find these climbs easy – there is frankly no substitute for experience here.[30]

These words increased the appeal of the Dubh Loch, adding yet another layer of intrigue onto the mysterious crag. The description seemed encouraging – I'm certainly not a honed strong man; my tendons are not made of rubber and my fingers are not pliers – but I didn't know whether I had the experience and technique required to pull it off. There was only one way to find out.

We begin.

From below, the first sequence had looked a little tedious: broken edges, grassy ledges, casual blocks. I assumed the real climbing would come later. However, once on, we discover that this sweeping assessment is wrong. The granite immediately tells us to open up. Look, think, feel. Pad with caution – wrap palms around a sloping corner – push down – curl fingers onto a chiselled line – press and reach. The granite demands full-bodied creativity.

Ahead, dark cracks beckon, promising security. But before reaching those safe enclaves, there is a delicate sequence to move through with care and precision.

Inhale: exhale. Survey the passage. An edge here to clasp; a bump there to reach for. And then, from the bump, another stretch across the blank slab before arrival at those distant

ledges. Feet? My feet will need to pad across the slab –
pressing down firm – trusting friction. There are no defined
scoops here.

This will be a little run-out. If I come off, I will swing in
a curving pendulum. If my gear holds.

We alternate leads and at the sharp end of the rope, I
discover the protection is sparse. Mixed. A little fiddly.

Many of the cracks turn out to be slightly awkward.
Shallow. Flared. Twisted. This is not like the deep spaces
that yawn open in rhyolite or limestone, welcoming solid
nut placements. The Dubh Loch cracks take thought and
ingenuity.

From my harness, I reach for an unusual set of nuts. Unlike
the standard oblong metal chocks that I have placed countless times, these have a curved wedge. I fiddle one into a
shallow groove, twisting and adjusting until it takes a sharp
tug. Tonight, when I shut my eyes and doze on the sofa, this
image will reappear sharply before me – a curved metal nut
slotted into a peculiar granite crack – quirky gear lodged
deep within some aspect of the mind.

———

Before I got on Cayman, my mind had run across it, trying
to anticipate what might unfold on that long granite wall.
This felt like an ambitious line – I was excited – but there
were also some stumbling blocks. Doubts and worries
niggled. Once we had ascertained that conditions were good
and most of the rock was dry, my concerns moved onto the
scale of the undertaking. Cayman was ten pitches of serious
granite climbing. Could I perform the piece?

Commitment wavers. I begin hesitant and uncertain.

Yet as we climb, passing up through one intricate pitch after another, the Dubh Loch pulls me into a new headspace. I see things differently. We are on the route now – committed – with finite time and energy. The longer we take, the slower we move, the harder things will become. This acceptance brings clarity and focus. The Dubh Loch tells me to climb. Climb well. Move efficiently.

Hesitation ceases.

Pushing and pulling, leaning down on ledges, bringing my toes up to stand beside my fingers, bridging out, lay-backing cracks: the granite invites the body to stretch and twist and reach. To span and bounce and balance. To lean into texture and walk up crystal walls.

The movement is three-dimensional and curiously intuitive.

Delicate traverses, round blocks, flared cracks and rough textures: this all feels familiar. Memories course through my muscles. Here, high in the Cairngorms, the gritstone returns. I remember that difficult grainy rock on those short wind-blasted Pennine edges and how it forced me to move in such particular ways. Back then those movements seemed desperately unnatural and I resented the rock for pushing me into wildly precarious positions.

Now, as I roll with the granite, all those difficult hours – all those rough physical tussles – shine in a new light. The pain, fear and frustration fade away, leaving something essential.

—

A peculiar intimacy develops between a climber and the rock. To some, it might look like an exercise in mastery: woman sets out to prove herself and conquer the mountain via the most difficult route possible. For some climbers, perhaps a checklist of achievements is all there is to it. But like moss or lichen, the more time I spend on rock, the more attached I grow to this stony matter.

An affinity for rock develops slowly. It is not something you can easily pin down, explain or quantify. It is an embodied knowledge, acquired through craft, care and practise. It is a relationship that is constantly evolving, developing and changing. In the process, for better or worse, the medium becomes engrained into your being. We shape the rock; the rock shapes us.

From hard, rounded gritstone to softly sculpted sandstone and razor-edged slate, the instinctive flow of rhyolite and commanding barbs of gabbro, in my journeys across the stones, I have shifted and melded, producing new shapes and adapting myself to fit around their forms. Climbing brings the rocks in, integrating the bones of the landscape within the human body. Sometimes I forget that this structure is part of me – sometimes I turn away from the rocks and leave off climbing for a while – but then something calls me back. Something reminds me, triggering that stony feeling, and then I long to be back moving among the rocks.

Climbing changes your relationship to landscape. The practice moves the mind, shifting thought away from the head and distributing it across other parts of the body. On the rock, I think through my hands, and over the years they have developed an intelligence that was never theirs before. Fingers are perceptive. They have learned to read the rock and they know how to handle it, feeling their way through the walls, seeking out the right hold to grasp and release.

The hands don't bear this work lightly. All the rough physical contact has changed them. My feet used to go through something similar each year when I spent summers scampering barefoot over sandy beaches and granite rocks. After a day of such tactile exploration, I loathed putting my shoes back on and instead would stubbornly trip up the rough track and hobble over gravel roads yowling with pain. At first those rough surfaces were unbearable, but over time the feet toughened up. With a thicker skin I could roam with greater ease, fitting my soles to the many textures, temperatures and qualities of the ground. Now my hands have taken on that close exploratory work and, like bare feet, they grow coarse and calloused but they also become more versatile, moving with greater confidence and tact, helping me come to know the land by hand.

But climbing is not just about the hands. The work invites a fluidity across the body – drawing many nerves and senses, muscles and limbs into play. On the rock, at some level, a climber is conscious at all times of where everything is, keeping tabs on the peripheries, noting which piece of matter each part of the body is leaning, resting, pulling or pushing against. Where once this intensity of body-knowledge was all-consuming and overwhelming, through practise and growing competence, I have learned to relax into this mode of awareness and have come to discover that this approach brings a distinctive understanding of place and self. Thinking through my entire body, I see the environment through an altered lens.

Moving through a rock face forces a climber to think

across multiple levels, holding many parts in play. Our minds run through our technical equipment, considering the rope and how it is running, placing gear to protect ourselves. We also think socially to collaborate on the rock. We work not just with our partner, but also with all the other non-human elements that we meet along the way. The rocks and moss, the weather and lichen, the light and anything or anyone else that might appear. Alert and responsive, the climber takes it all in, balancing up a great assemblage of information to navigate the dynamic rock face.

In coming to grips with this craft, I have sought to take things further. Widening the perspective – moving beyond equipment, technique and climbing culture – other histories and cultures come into play. Moving with a rock face can bring a sense of rounded encapsulation. Within the embodied climbing moment, we handle many facets and aspects of a place reaching towards a grasp of the total environment.

——

Our line on the Dubh Loch takes us into a world of intricate complexity. We must stay attentive and keep flexible. Things are constantly changing.

We began on sun-kissed rock. Then – in a transition as striking as an eclipse – the sun leaves us. The Dubh Loch faces east: the Earth has turned and from this point onwards, we are destined to climb in the shadow of the mountain. The temperature drops. Muscles contract. Fingers threaten to turn stony. Wind gusts and sudden blasts catch us mid-move, forcing us to breathe harder, pulling air down into our lungs.

The granite must be tested. Wind, water and ice pick at the surface, teasing out gaps, opening cracks and loosening flakes. I hit suspect blocks with the heel of my palm, listening closely to the acoustics. If the thud reverberates, a hollow note rings out. Then I tread carefully. The climber's movement across the vertical landscape is a sensitive performance.

Unlike the conclusive choreography of a boulder problem, such long, remote mountain routes have an enigmatic structure. The piece extends, rolling out through a huge sweep of landscape composed of many beginnings and endings – or pointed moments and sequences – shaping our lengthy passage in and out of the mountain.

At the crux wall, the body tenses, flying up through an imposing black roof to meet a steep face bristling with black moss. Here the entire piece could come undone but the plants are miraculously dry and a surge of strength and determination sees us through.

Later, when we eventually top out onto the summit plain, our limbs will slump into the pillowed mosses and lichens while the eyes roam out across the plateau, briefly taking in the undulating hill and cloudscape, before turning away from the bracing blast of unbroken wind, remembering that this point is far from the end.

We will drop back down the boulder-choked gully and then walk out, another three- or four-hour route following the mountain watercourses on a passage that will see the day through, from dusk into darkness. First the bats emerge, flitting between the darkening trees, then the stars come out and later we will hear stags roaring into the night. There are many shades and tones to the mountain performance.

Even once we are off the mountain, the piece will continue

to make itself felt in a ravenous hunger, the sleep of the dead and a spell of whole body exhaustion that lasts several days, leaving that disorienting sensation that the mountain has left its mark, touching, at times, on a sense of loss, as though something has been left behind on that great face.

——

Meanwhile, still inside the climb, the day rolls on, time passing in that peculiar way of a long rock climb. Seconds swell, expanding to carry the full significance of a moment while the hours disappear, unnoticed, lost inside the granite dream space.

Gravity tugs at my body, the pull growing stronger as we near the top.

Some 400 million years ago, all this material was molten magma cooling deep within the Earth; 400 million years in the future, it will all be gone. The Dubh Loch will break down and wash away, the particles moving on through the rock cycle, perhaps turning up as a new sand or gritstone that eventually sinks back down into the Earth to be melted and cooked into some new form.

Within such big rhythms, I am next to nothing.

I lean back into the rock, pulling away from the wind to shelter beside a small rowan tree – its trunk no thicker than my little finger – perched high in a remote enclave on the cliff face. The rowan's green feathered leaves are just starting to turn, burning fiery-red at the tips. Soon those leaves will drop away and my companion will weather out the winter storms, buried in snow, encased in ice, waiting for the return of the brief growing season.

Together, we look out over a sweeping vista – below, the ruffling black loch, and beyond, swatches of heathered hills stretching out under hazy-blue autumn skies.

When I was a child, I once lay on my back, looking up at the sky, trying to see the Earth move. From that position, the sky grew and I had a strange worldly sensation – that the surface of this planet was much bigger than I had previously known. Pinned to the grass, with a sickening rush, I saw how small I was. For the first time, I grasped that life – so many lives – had gone before my own and so many would come after. Suddenly, I saw that my place in the world was unfathomably tiny. I saw that my own individual consciousness – my ability to see, to know, to think, to feel, to love – was a momentary blip; that my existence was a brief window within a dizzying expanse of space and life and time. The universe had appeared: I had lost my position at the centre.

The thought fascinated and terrified me. I stayed with it for as long as I could bear – feeling as though I was on a roller coaster racing into the heart of some unfathomable mystery – then I fidgeted, got up and ran away to stick my head into smaller earthly matters.

From minute material details to dizzying expanses of space and time, climbing has helped me to move more fluently between some of the vastly differing scales of existence. On the rock face, I move with the landscape, following its many rhythms and natures, tuning into lives big and small, past, present and future.

—

High on the Dubh Loch I tire, but still the granite asks more of me, still presenting manifold openings, each calling for more strength and grace. A corner to bridge and balance across. Cracks into which the fingers slide, twist and expand. A sloping face to pull and pad upon. Through these features, I give my weight to the granite, distributing my mass, now here and now there, letting the rock take my form as I take on its form.

The self is poured into the stone and the rock flows through the body.

In this state of being, boundaries loosen. Things lose their solidity. A surface becomes an opening. Rocks gain depth, history and character. The human body and the material world meet and mingle in a shifting play of selves.

From the rock face, where a climbing body plunges in and out of ancient matter, things feel different. Reaching into the core – in these moments of searing intimacy – the world reveals itself. Nothing is static. This place is an immense unfolding of dazzling vitality.

ACKNOWLEDGEMENTS

Many wonderful people helped to make this book and I am beyond grateful for all the support and friendship I have been given along the way.

The climbing community has been a constant source of strength and I am indebted to all of those who have shared their enthusiasm, knowledge and good humour with me. Variously acting as teachers, mentors, partners and friends, these people have helped me find my way into the culture and practice of rock climbing, opening my eyes to the magic of the pursuit. Special thanks to Andrew Veal, Anta Misina, Ben Watson, Bill Birkett, Daniel Moore, Helen Mort, Jules Lines, Luke Perry, Rob Greenwood, Will Boyd-Wallis, Zoe Strong, Mercian Mountaineering Club, Moray Mountaineering Club and the Jacobites.

Simone Kenyon introduced me to the world of dance and performing art, welcoming me into the brilliant Into the Mountain company when they began their performance journey in the Cairngorms. Thanks to all the women within that project and all those I have met since who have given the most beautiful insights into place, self, body and movement. I am grateful to Rebecca Collins, Kate Lawrence, Branwen Davies, Neil Callaghan and Keren Smail.

A number of people read drafts and extracts of this book as it developed, offering quality feedback and much-needed encouragement. As well as those already named, thanks to Bronagh Gallagher, Rosie Vincent, Ryan Dziadowiec and the Cumberland Arms writing group. Fiona McGibbon made an excellent geology teacher, guiding me into the dizzying timescales and terminology of the science and I am grateful to have had her expert eye check over the finished manuscript. Carl McKeating and Rachel Crolla played an invaluable role in the formation of this project – they also helped to see it through to the finish. Thanks to John Whale for his discerning perspective on the manuscript. And Steffan Gwynn, housemate and sounding board par excellence, *diolch yn fawr*.

I'm grateful to my agent James MacDonald Lockhart for taking such a keen interest in this project and helping to make it happen. The Society of Authors provided a generous grant. Jacquie Macintyre and Katie Crerar gave me space to write and play in the mountains in the summer and Sian Jamieson very kindly gave me a home for the winter. Thanks to my editor Simon Thorogood, Aa'Ishah Hawton and the team at Canongate for sharing my enthusiasm and nurturing this book into existence.

Finally, my friends and family have given endless love and encouragement. This book is dedicated to all of you.

NOTES AND REFERENCES

1   Joe Brown, *The Hard Years* (London: Phoenix, 1967), p. 33

2   Gwen Moffatt, *Space Below My Feet* (London: Phoenix, 2013), p. 7

3   Chris Bonington, *Ascent: A Life Spent Climbing on the Edge* (London: Simon & Schuster, 2012), p. 31

4   Brown, *The Hard Years*, p. 42

5   'Life in North Kerry', *The Wheels of the World*, RTÉ, first broadcast 4 November 1974. Available at   https://www.rte.ie/archives/exhibitions/2257-on-the-farm/642537-life-in-north-kerry/ [accessed 13 July 2021]

6   Dave Musgrove (ed), *Yorkshire Gritstone* (Dewsbury: Yorkshire Mountaineering Club, 1998), p. 530

7   Musgrove (ed), *Yorkshire Gritstone*, p. 13

8   Emily Brontë, *Wuthering Heights* (Oxford: Oxford University Press, 2009), p. 72

9   Brontë, *Wuthering Heights*, p. 29

10   However, the early Alpinists were disdainful of this practice: when the Climbers' Club was formed in 1897, the president of the older Alpine Club (founded 1857) denounced it as a 'A Climber's Club for "chimney sweeps"'. See Simon Thompson, *Unjustifiable Risk? The Story of British Climbing* (Milnthorpe: Cicerone, 2012), p. 92

11   From Fawkes's speech to the House of Commons on the Bill: 'Let us not go forth with the wrongs of Africa as a weight upon our hearts; but rather let us rid our country of the sin, and in the passing

of this act of legislative wisdom and justice, make some atonement for the too-long injured and insulted rights of humanity.' Walter Fawkes, Commons Address, 23 February 1807. Available at: https://api.parliament.uk/historic-hansard/commons/1807/feb/23/slave-trade-abolition-bill [Accessed 1 July 2020]

12 Figures from 'Henry Lascelles, 2nd Earl of Harewood', Centre for the Study of the Legacies of British Slavery, University College London, Available at: https://www.ucl.ac.uk/lbs/person/view/6180 [Accessed 14 July 2021]

13 An analysis of 1,382 sport and exercise research studies conducted between 2011 and 2013 shows that of 6 million participants, only 39 per cent were women (G. Bruinvels, R.J. Burden, A.J. McGregor, et al, 'Sport, exercise and the menstrual cycle: where is the research?', *British Journal of Sports Medicine* 51 (2017) pp. 487–8

14 See the TED talk by Dr Tracy Sims, *Women are not Small Men* (2019), where Sims gives an overview of the history of research into women's bodies and the menstrual cycle and how to apply female-specific nutrition and training plans to exercise. A 2019 article in the *Washington Post* outlines how athletes are using emerging research into the menstrual cycle to help them compete. (Amanda Loudin, 'New research on the menstrual cycle and athletic performance helps women compete', *Washington Post*, 19 October 2019, available at: https://www.washingtonpost.com/health/an-athletic-life-vs-that-time-of-the-month-new-research-is-helping-female-athletes-compete/2019/10/18/523fe92a-dfb2-11e9-be96-6adb81821e90_story.html [Accessed 29 July 2021]). Another 2019 article on the BBC Sport website shows how football teams and coaches are developing training plans in line with the female hormonal cycle (Amy Lofthouse, 'Periods – how do they affect athletes & why are they monitored?', BBC Sport, 21 May 2019, https://www.bbc.co.uk/sport/48243310 [Accessed 29 July 2021])

15 Sorley MacLean, *An Cuilithionn* (Glasgow: Association for Scottish Literary Studies, 2011), ll. 92–7, p. 102

16 A 'river' is the Cumbrian term for the person who split the slate stones into thin slices for dressing

17 Bill Peascod and Bill Birkett, *Women Climbing: 200 Years of Achievement* (London: A & C Black, 1989), p. 11

18 Ibid.

19 Lawrence Pilkington, 'The Inaccessible Pinnacle', *Scottish Mountaineering Club Journal* 22 (April 1939), p. 63

20 Simon Richardson, 'Quoth the Raven – Nevermore', Scottishwinter. com, 9 December 2020, available at http://www.scottishwinter. com/?p=7471 [Accessed 15 July 2021]

21 Nan Shepherd, *The Living Mountain* (Edinburgh: Canongate, 2011), p. 106

22 In the 1960s, Leeds University left their hallmark on crags around the UK with route names including Depravity, Lust, Necrophilia, Bestiality and Debauchery. Through the Black Lives Matter movement there was a call to re-examine route names in America, where racism is written into the rock. Equality in the outdoors is a long way off when routes are still named Happiness in Slavery, Neck in the Noose, Whipping Post and Slant Eyes.

23 The ancient Celtic language, once spoken widely across Europe, now lingers in two distinct branches. Welsh, Cornish and Breton are the P-Celtic languages. Irish, Scottish Gaelic and Manx are the Q-Celtic languages, whose ancient speakers could not pronounce the 'p' sound and so substituted that sound with the harder 'q'. Modern-day speakers of P- and Q-Celtic will struggle to understand one another as the languages have changed and moved further apart over the last two thousand years.

24 Shepherd, *The Living Mountain*, p. 108.

25 Ibid.

26 Tom Patey, 'Cairngorm Commentary', in *One Man's Mountains* (Edinburgh: Canongate, 1997), pp. 66–81 (p. 66)

27 Nan Shepherd writes that the granite 'weathers too smoothly and squarely to make the best conditions for rock-climbing'. Shepherd, *The Living Mountain*, p. 4

28 Jim Bell and Bill Murray quoted in Greg Strange, *The Cairngorms: 100 Years of Mountaineering* (Leicester: Scottish Mountaineering Trust, 2010), p. 50

29 Strange, *The Cairngorms*, pp. 55–9

30 Jules Lines in Guy Robertson (ed.), *The Great Mountain Crags of Scotland* (Sheffield: Vertebrate, 2014), p. 279